Growing Spirituality

Growing towards one another
by journeying in the footsteps of Christ.

Cameron Butland

Open Spirituality Publishing

Cameron Butland is a member of the Cumbria Ecumenical Spirituality Group and is Carlisle Diocesan Spirituality Adviser. He speaks regularly on various topics including: 'Celtic Spirituality', 'Desert Fathers and Mothers', 'Contemplative Living', and 'Christian Meditation'. Over the last nine years he has been part of the team leading the yearlong 'Nourishing the Soul' course, which is an introduction to Christian spirituality. In addition he has taken part in delivering the last two 'Training Spiritual Directors' courses for Cumbria. He is the Bishop of Carlisle's Chaplain.

Previous books:
'Work in Worship'
'Walking into Celtic Spirituality'

Open Spirituality Publishing
© Copyright Cameron Butland, 2017
ISBN 978-0-9926277-1-3

Printed by Book Printing UK
Remus House, Coltsfoot Drive, Peterborough, PE2 9BF

*This book is dedicated to all my friends
in the Cumbria Ecumenical Spirituality Group.*

*Thank you for all you have taught me
and so many others over the past eight years.*

Preface

In January 2016, Methodist District Chairman Richard Teal asked me to write a few notes about the formation of *The Ecumenical County of Cumbria*. Chapter 1 of this book was largely the result. Having written this, I realised that there was so much more that could be said. This book is a personal reflection on the journey of faith that has brought us to this point. This is the culmination of the last eight years working as part of the Cumbria Ecumenical Spirituality Group. This book is dedicated to my colleagues whom I have worked with on a variety of courses and events and from whom I have learnt so much. I am also indebted to those who have attended events that the group has organised, especially the 'Nourishing the Soul' and 'Introduction to Spiritual Direction' yearlong courses. The growth in numbers wanting to be part of these courses and in those seeking spiritual direction has proved to be the most encouraging part of my ministry.

I am keen to acknowledge the support that I have received from all the denominational leaders in Cumbria. It is my great fortune to be employed as the Bishop of Carlisle's chaplain; Bishop James has given me a unique double role in the diocese which gives me an overview of all that is happening. The relationships formed by the ecumenical county and the encouragement of not only Richard Teal but also Sarah Moore and Drew McCombe have been extremely helpful.

Most of all, I acknowledge the hundreds of people who in all our churches are making the ecumenical county a reality. Cumbria is an exciting place to be, seeing not just the churches but also faith itself coming alive again in people and communities. If Cumbria can act as template for anywhere else, it is in this spirit of revival in those being drawn into faith and those being called into service.

Contents

Growing Spirituality

Chapter One
On being an ecumenical county

The context
Cumbria has a long history of ecumenical cooperation. The geographical size of the present county and its limited transport infrastructure give its communities strong local identities. Until 1974, the present unified county was split into three—Cumberland, Lancashire and Westmorland. Those old boundaries still influence many attitudes and are still difficult to cross psychologically. In addition, there are proud local identities to do with established industry and commercial activity. So Barrow is associated with shipbuilding, much of the west coast with the nuclear power industry, and the centre of the county with tourism since the 1850s.

All of this makes 'local' very important, so churches identify themselves with places more often than with denominations. Over the last thirty years, there have been places where churches have simply worked together and developed a mosaic of local ecumenical partnerships that are informal and non-structural. Shared fairs, carol singers, lunches for the elderly and village festivals like Rushbearing are communal activities that are often used as ways of expressing local unity. It is significant that where the present proposed Mission Community[1] builds upon these local partnerships, this appears to be an almost natural evolution.

---

[1] 'Mission community' is the term for the local groupings of churches and congregations that are co-operating together to share mission, ministry and buildings. They can be large in population, in area or in the number of churches. It is estimated that there will be around thirty-five formed across Cumbria.

This natural focus towards the 'local' also causes problems due to the intense rivalry between communities. I could give examples, but I want to continue working in the county, so I better not!

In general terms, the geography of Cumbria and its localism are the key foundations for the ecumenical county. In ecclesial terms, it is fortunate that the Anglican Diocese, Methodist District and United Reformed Church Area are almost co-terminus. In addition, the lack of many neighbouring counties means that Cumbria cannot easily look beyond its boundaries. Recent experience suggests that even those other counties on our borders do not look to Cumbria but rather away from it to larger population centres. There are, though, other parts of Britain which experience similar isolation and localism, so why is it that Cumbria became the first ecumenical county? 'Relational ecumenism' is the key to understanding the developments in Cumbria. Our ecumenism begins not with shared doctrine, or managing decline, but rather, seeing in each other a fellow child of God. Good relationships brought about the ecumenical county, and they will be the most important factor in the success of our common mission.

First Steps
In 1999, for the millennium celebration, the then church leaders of Cumbria signed a common declaration of faith and a commitment to pray together. This was a bringing together of a great deal of ecumenical work that had happened over the previous twenty years, including the formation of churches together. Churches had also worked together on the Five Marks of Mission, growing healthy churches and local missions. The year 1999, though, marked the first sustained attempt to bring the church leaders together to give a united voice to the

ecumenical cooperation that was evident at a local level. The first major flooding in a generation in 2005 which affected communities in Carlisle and Kendal, brought the local churches together, working with the local authorities to assist victims and to support rescue services. The lessons learnt at this time, as well as the friendships made, not only assisted in responding to the flooding of 2009 and 2015, but also became a permanent way of working together.

The relationship of praying communities also shouldn't be ignored. Whilst local churches praying together might seem unremarkable compared to the big initiatives of the last five years, the impact of the church leaders being seen to pray together in 1999 encouraged many congregations to follow this example, and in many places, Christians came together regularly to pray in January, Lent, Pentecost and at Harvest to have joint prayer groups and services. Personally arriving in Cumbria in 2004, I was struck, as Chaplain of Rydal Hall, by the many descriptions of the way local Christians regularly prayed together. Another significant factor in the county had been the work done by David and Sheila Wood in promoting prayer groups based on the practice of Benedictine silent prayer. The importance of praying together and for each other shouldn't be underestimated in what has followed.

At the same time, the national programme of discussions between the denominations also had an impact upon Cumbria. The Methodist and URC churches began local conversations about pooling resources and ministry, regularly meeting together and praying before the first formal conversations in 2008.

Tripartite Conversations

Whilst relationships among the church leaders had been very good for many years, it was the appointment of three new leaders that gave the ecumenical county its voice. Within the space of three years, the URC North West Synod appointed Rachel Poolman as Cumbria Area Moderator, the Cumbria Methodist District appointed the Reverend Richard Teal as Chairman, and the Anglican Diocese of Carlisle had a new bishop, the Right Reverend James Newcome. All three had considerable experience in ecumenical working and a shared enthusiasm for churches working together. It was of considerable added benefit that Bishop James had previously been Bishop of Penrith and so had considerable experience of the county.

Formal discussions began between the Methodist District and URC Cumbria Area in 2008. Shortly after these initial discussions, the Venerable George Howe asked to be involved on behalf of the Diocese of Carlisle. In 2009, the formal talks were reconstituted to be a three-way conversation between the three denominations. Each denomination had three members— the church leader plus two others—and the nine representatives were facilitated by an independent co-ordinator, the Reverend Ruth Harvey. The aim of the discussions was to produce a simple, clear and understandable covenant that would provide a viable way of the churches working visibly together. The Tripartite Group prayed together at all their meetings, and from the first, there was a strong common purpose in working together, which led to a basis of trust. The contribution made by Ruth Harvey in making the process work proved to be invaluable, and in many ways, her skilled facilitation enabled the group to make more rapid progress that might have been otherwise possible.

The second major flooding of Cumbria in recent years took place as the Tripartite discussions were ongoing. Building on the experience of the floods four years previous, the response of the churches was more organised and brought praise both in the county and nationally. The proactive nature of the churches in housing and feeding flood victims, providing prayer and emotional support and simply being able to mobilise so many volunteers in the space of a few hours made an impact not just directly in Keswick, Cockermouth, Workington and Carlisle, but also to the churches themselves. In addition, the church leaders were able to be visible in a way not possible previously; to see the leaders together was a bold statement of a united church. The church leaders were able to speak with one voice, and this was even more evident in 2010 when, in the aftermath of the Derek Bird shootings, the three leaders stood side by side with the families of the victims. These are powerful images in a shared mission to the county, and these pivotal moments marked a new depth to the ecumenical sharing between the churches. The impact of the events in 2009 and 2010 forged many of the relationships between individuals which are, seven years later, driving the ecumenical county.

In 2009, the Cumbria Ecumenical Spirituality Group (CESG) was also formed. This grouping brought together those who were seeking to offer teaching in prayer and encouraged those within the churches, as well as on its fringes, to renew their spiritual lives. The individuals who formed the group brought a wide experience from outside the county and were members of the three denominations. From the first, all the events and prayer materials were ecumenical in nature. The response to the prayer days in 2010 was overwhelming, with over seventy people attending the first day at Rydal Hall in October. The first members of CESG attempted to make contact and work with all those already encouraging prayer in the county. This foundation of prayer and the rapid development of spiritual learning have been some of the unseen factors in supporting the creation of an ecumenical county. CESG, from its inception, met with the three church leaders and was adopted by Churches Together in Cumbria (CTiC), reporting annually to its executive council and producing a summary for the CTiC annual report.

Declaration of the Ecumenical County

The Tripartite conversations in 2011 reached agreement in three areas: shared mission, common ministry and imaginative use of buildings. These key principles were carefully worded into the statement 'Ecumenical County of Cumbria: A Declaration of Intent by the Methodist, United Reformed and Anglican Churches'. The wording of this statement was painstakingly prepared, taken to the three denominational synods, checked out with national church bodies and eventually agreed. The signing by the three denominational leaders on Advent Sunday— November 27, 2011—marked the end of one chapter and the beginning of a new one. However, the significance of this moment of signing shouldn't be underestimated. Not only did the three denominational leaders, Bishop James, Richard Teal and Richard Church (for the URC, as Rachel Poolman moved to the northeast just before the signing), sign, but also five companion denominations were in attendance. The presence of church leaders from the Roman Catholic Diocese of Lancaster, Church of Scotland, Salvation Army, Society of Friends and Baptist churches lent real credibility to this being an ecumenical county. The only omissions from the Christian family were representatives of the free and independent churches, but representatives of these churches now also meet with the other denominational leaders annually for prayer and discussion.

Whilst the signing of the declaration marked a significant moment of coming together, it also gave rise to many anxieties.

Each of the three denominations already had their programmes of the mission, and these needed to be brought together. In addition, there were significant obstacles to be overcome for a shared ministry. The audit of the use of the buildings was, by comparison, considerably easier than the first two commitments, even though it was a daunting task to survey six hundred buildings. It was to be expected that following the signing, there was some frustration and irritation that little seemed to be happening. This was unsurprising, given that there were already twenty-seven places which either had an LEP or some other form of sharing agreement, and of course, it is easy not to understand the complexity of a whole ecumenical county as opposed to a simple local arrangement.

Having brought about the signing of the declaration, the Tripartite Group offered to disband. However, it was reconstituted and changed its name to the Growing Together Group. Its role remains to pray together, to hold the vision of the ecumenical county, to encourage other denominations to join and to address issues of principle.

Small steps towards the bigger vision
Despite the first work being done on the buildings' audit, the first significant step was the development of the ministry strategy. This focused on how the ministry could be shared. The twin strategies of the Mission Communities and forming a Covenant Partnership in an Extended Area (CPEA) arose from this consultation. The bold statement in the declaration 'to work together, to equip both lay and ordained ministry whenever possible and to share that ministry wherever appropriate'[2] now

---

[2] *Ecumenical County of Cumbria: A Declaration of Intent* by the Methodist, United Reformed and Anglican Churches, signed November 27, 2011.

took a practical form. This proved a shock to some and an encouragement to others. All three synods considered the strategy, and local churches were asked to consider its implications. The responses proved to be so varied and complicated that a new ecumenical task group had to be formed to manage all the comments, suggestions and objections.

The work done by this group from 2013 to 2014 was significant; by listening to every viewpoint and acknowledging what was said, the group gradually allowed everyone to begin to see the strategy as their own. There were some areas of resistance and apathy that remained, but the vast majority of the churches proved to be supportive. Despite a sceptical series of synods in 2013, by October 2014, all the three denominations had agreed to form Mission Communities; by 2020, all churches would be a part of one of about thirty-five groupings. Of course, this was a huge undertaking, and to facilitate this, the Strategy Steering Group was formed from an enlarged membership of the task group. Under the chairmanship of the Right Reverend Robert Freeman (successor to Bishop James as Bishop of Penrith), this ecumenical group is co-ordinating the development of the ecumenical county.

The CPEA has now been agreed and implemented. On November 27, 2016 in Carlisle Cathedral, Bishop James Newcome, The Reverend Richard Teal, The Reverend Sarah Moore and Major Drew McCombe – the representatives of the four partner denominations signed the declaration:

'With the whole Christian Church, we believe in one God, Father, Son and Holy Spirit.
'We share a life of faith which is the Spirit's gift, continually received through the Word, the Sacraments and our Christian life together.

Growing Spirituality

'We believe that we are being called by God to realise more deeply our common life and mission, to share and respect the distinctive contributions of our traditions, and to bring about closer collaboration in all areas of witness and service.
'We commit ourselves and our churches:
a. to seek out every possible opportunity for joint initiatives, especially God for All, at local and county level in mission to all the people of Cumbria.
b. to work together to equip both lay and ordained ministry whenever possible, and to share that ministry wherever appropriate.
c. to continue the work of developing strategies whereby we optimise the use of our church buildings for the benefit of communities throughout the county.

'We believe that God has given our four churches a particular opportunity to work together more closely.
'We adopt together a Covenant Partnership in Extended Area (CPEA) to allow sharing of ministry as appropriate in view of our traditions.
'We also affirm our intention to go on praying and working, with all our fellow Christians, for the visible unity of the Church in the way Christ chooses, so that people may be led to love and serve God more and more'.[3]

In making the ecumenical county a reality, these steps are fundamental; local groupings now have the freedom and permission to work together in a shared ministry and mission.

---

[3] *A Declaration of Covenant Partnership* by the Church of England, Methodist Church, Salvation Army and United Reformed Church.

The first Mission Community was commissioned in January 2016, and by the end of 2017, an estimated eighteen will have been launched. There remain seemingly intractable problems in five to six areas, but it is hugely encouraging that so many churches are so supportive. In terms of the two key steps, the CPEA attracted support across the three denominations of over 95 percent of the churches. A few churches have, for a variety of reasons, wished to opt out; in these cases, arrangements are being made for variation in membership of an associational nature, but eventually, all will have some kind of missional relationship with its Mission Community.

Mission - the heartbeat of the ecumenical county
In 2010, the Diocese of Carlisle launched its vision and strategy document 'Growing Disciples'. Much of this statement was written in ecumenical terms, and the other denominations echoed the missional intent expressed. However, the forming of the ecumenical county required a common statement of intent. The 'God for All' umbrella process was adopted to express this coming together in 2014. Initially, this led to some confusion, but the church leaders (via a road show around the county), internal communications, and synod debates got the message across that God for All was bringing together all the missional activity already happening but, at the same time, providing more resources.

One of the issues about the ecumenical county from the beginning was inequality in terms of size, finances and geographical spread among the three denominations. The larger size of the Anglican diocese could have proved to be an obstacle to the ecumenical county, being seen as an Anglican takeover. Whilst there have been tensions on all sides, the remarkable feature is that all three denominations have worked together with reasonable equanimity. Offence can be caused by denominations seeming to forget about their ecumenical partners. Frustration can also result in from what seem as unnecessary delays caused by ecumenical consultation. Given the scope for difficulties caused by the different ecclesiologies of the three denominations and their distinctive bureaucratic committee structures, the surprising thing is that the ecumenical county hasn't come to a halt under this burden. Two things, though, have made a difference; at each development, the ecumenical county has been rooted in prayer. Prayers have been encouraged at each stage, and the publication of prayers has helped to root each step. Secondly, the personal relationships formed have cut through red tape and looked for what is possible. That the ecumenical county is rapidly becoming a reality in our churches and communities is a powerful sign of the Holy Spirit at work.

In 2014, the diocese formed the Reach Team. The Anglican Synod agreed to fund posts to provide a resource to the newly forming MCs. The reach understanding of the mission speaks in four directions—Me, In, Out and Big:
- 'Me' Reach is about the individual's own spirituality, the way in which we come alive to God in our prayer and faith;
- 'In' Reach is the desire to make the life of our churches more accessible to seekers;
- 'Out' Reach is the activity of the church in proclaiming the good news of Jesus outside our normal activities; and
- 'Big' Reach is the proclamation of the Gospel in big events and in the big world of social media and the web.

The members of the Reach Team bring a wealth of experience of missional activity and ecumenism. A Methodist minister joined them in 2015, and an agreement has been reached for the appointment of a post funded by the Methodist District for a digital evangelist. This will add significant expertise and resource.

The ecumenical county has now developed three characteristics. It seeks to grow disciples, to provide a Christian presence in every community and to proclaim God for All. In pursuing these aims, the commitment of all the churches is to reach every person living in Cumbria by 2020 (the population currently being 496,200).

Ongoing developments
The result of the building audit was published in October 2015. The report demonstrated the variety of purposes the buildings of the three denominations were being used for, but it also now leads to decisions about what is the best way forward. Crucial to this discussion are the mixed blessings of the historic buildings, mostly in the diocese which are costly to maintain and of limited value as a community resource. In 2015, the General Synod suggested that some historic churches might become 'festival churches', and this suggests one way forward, but the local decisions will be made on the basis of the missional strategy of each Mission Community.

In 2014, the training partnership between Carlisle and Blackburn was put on notice that it would not continue beyond the summer of 2016. Blackburn was withdrawing and looking south to form another partnership. This left the diocese in Cumbria with a dilemma. At a time of ambitious expansion of lay and ordained training, the main vehicle for its delivery was breaking up. The training provided by the companion denominations had been centralised by the national church, and this was a major threat to the viability of Mission Communities. The diocese decided to form a different style of educational programme that would encompass all forms of training and discipleship. The Cumbria

Christian Learning (CCL) programme had been created as a result and came into being on September 1, 2016. It is to be hoped that it will be able to work ecumenically and at a local level in the Mission Communities, there is a great deal of development work still to be done.

Prayer—the first, the last and in all things

The ecumenical county was born out of church leaders praying together. The growth of prayer across the county is one of the most encouraging signs. The sharing of spirituality and prayer among the companion denominations is developing beyond the capacity of any one grouping or denomination to facilitate. Prayer is at the root of all that is being done in the name of the ecumenical county. The next years will be a time of exciting change which will of course be unnerving to some but for the majority mean the deepening of their own spirituality which will lead them to understand the ecumenical county in a richer way. In so doing, we will all become more missional, and each will be prepared 'to give account of the good news that is within us'. Together we will find a greater depth of meaning in our common life, and the challenges we face are nothing compared to the opportunity being presented to us to show the love of God, for as Jesus prayed 'by this will, all know that they are my disciples'.

SECTION A
OUR COMMON ROOTS

In this section, the story of the first Christians in Cumbria is told.

Chapter 2 describes the involvement of Ninian and Patrick in Cumbria's story in the fifth century. It describes Kentigern's involvement in the sixth century and then that of Oswald and Aidan in the seventh century. Lastly, looking briefly at the legacy of Cuthbert and Bega, as well as Bede's witness, this chapter discusses their unique contribution to the founding of the church in the county.

Chapter 3 highlights the suffering of the Norman Conquest for Cumbria and the dislocation of the social fabric. It traces the founding of the great religious houses of prayer in the thirteenth, fourteenth and fifteenth centuries. The legacy of the Augustinians and Benedictines is to be recognised not just in the ruined abbeys of the present landscapes but also, much more importantly, in the foundation of contemplative prayer.

Chapter 4 draws out in discussion the common roots of the present churches in Cumbria. Three central principles are proposed. The Christian roots are to be found in
- Christian unity;
- prayer as a way of living; and
- instinctive mission.

Chapter Two
The first Christians

When we look at the past, the present age gets in the way. This is obvious, but it is worth saying at the beginning. We struggle to understand the distant past because it is overlaid by the generations who have come after and whose concerns obscure the different world of our ancestors. However, two things for us always remain the same—people and faith. Our ancestors are like us; they need food, water, heat and shelter, and they love, have families and grieve. Our ancestors may appear different from us, but their DNA is part of us, and their daily needs are the same as ours. More than this, for modern Christians, we can often recognise their patterns of behaviour, because we too share the motivations of faith. So if we are to ask, 'Who were the first Christians in what we now call Cumbria?' we already know some of the answers in the way we live in faith.

Who was the first Christian to live in this land of lakes, mountains and the wild coast? No one can possibly know, but what we do know is that people lived in Cumbria at the time Christianity came to the Roman province of Britain. We also have a record that there were two deacons living in the city of Carlisle in the third century. The constant changeover of troops at Hadrian's Wall must have made third-century Cumbria a vibrant place to live. Often, the borderlands contain some of the most dynamic groups of people in any society, and this must have been true for the melting pot of the lands on both sides of the Roman Wall. Originally conceived as a defensive barrier, it became, by the end of the third century, the centre of trade between the Roman and non-Roman world.

The Edict of Milan in 313 changed the place of faith within the Roman Empire. Often cited as making the empire Christian, in truth, Constantine's Edict was a more open and tolerant declaration. Christianity, amongst many other religions, was to be tolerated so long as it did not conflict with the bureaucracies of the imperial state. Only later did the emperor himself profess his own Christianity. The Christian Church had been persecuted for most of the previous generation but, after 313, was found to have been growing as an underground movement which then flourished in the fourth century. Its influence and membership grew dramatically throughout the century; as the challenges grew in the Roman Empire, increasingly, Christianity became its distinctive legacy in Western Europe.

Ninian the Founder
For Cumbria the earliest person that the Christian story can go back to is Ninian. From Ninian, we can trace the growth of Christian influence on the communities of Cumbria. He was probably born fifty years after the Edict of Milan. So he would have been born in a world where the Roman Empire was Christian but facing financial and organisational challenges. The external threats were becoming more pressing, and the old certainties were rapidly being lost. Ninian was perhaps born in Galloway, north of the Roman Wall; his birth place is assumed due to that the fact that he was said to have returned to his home when he founded his community at Whithorn. Ninian travelled to Rome for his Christian education and ordination, returning via the community at Marmoutier. It is not known exactly when he came to Whithorn, but it would have been close to the beginning of the fifth century, just as the Pax Romana was about to break down in Britain. In 410, the three Roman legions were withdrawn to defend the Rhine border, and in that moment, Roman Britain began its long decline.

Ninian's community flourished at Whithorn, drawing admirers and students from across Europe. At Whithorn in 451, the earliest known Christian inscription in Britain was carved on a gravestone, but who Latinus was and why he was important enough to have his own stone is unclear. What is obvious, though, is the opening words of his inscription: 'Te Deum laudemus'. Here was a lively Christian community where those who died were celebrated for their faith.

It seems likely that Cumbria was the home of Patrick. There are several places associated with Ireland's patron saint in the county. Although some claim Patrick has Welsh origins, it seems much more likely that he comes from Cumbria. He was kidnapped probably a few years after Ninian had set up his community at Whithorn. The beginning of the fifth century was a time of intense raiding from the tribes of Ulster, as the coast was no longer defended by the Roman fleet. It seems entirely reasonable that Patrick, as the son of Christian deacon Calpornius, was snatched as a slave of the Uí Néill clan from a beach on the Solway Firth, overlooked by the hill, to which his ashes would return in 461, now known as Aspatria (an abbreviation of its ancient name 'The Ashes of St Patrick').

Ninian and Patrick were both educated in Rome. They were ordained in Rome and held commissions as missionaries. They were, though, evangelists of the Christian Church. Many histories speak foolishly of the Roman Church, the British Church and the Celtic Church. All these terms are inventions of later generations. Ninian and Patrick only recognised one Church, united by one Baptism, a community of disciples of one Lord and faithful to the books of the good news of Jesus. These books which were for the first time authorised as sacred scripture by the great council of Laodicea in 363, were known to Ninian and Patrick. Of all the new books of the bible, though, the one simply titled 'according to John' was regarded as the most important. St. Antony the Great had died in 356, but his influence on the early Constantine church of the fourth century was immense. Growing up under the persecution of Diocletian, he had known only John's Gospel (the word 'Gospel' was devised by the authors of the King James Bible in 1611). St. Antony's devotion to Jesus, as presented in the Gospel of John, was fundamental to the prayer tradition of the desert fathers and mothers. In turn, the conversations with John Cassien, with the Abbas and Ammas of the desert tradition, were held dear by St. Martin at Marmoutier. Ninian not only brought with him from Marmoutier the stone masons who built Candida Casa (Latin for 'White House', from which the present name Whithorn comes), but also a way of praying in creation rooted in St. Antony's teaching. St. Antony told all those who came to him in the desert to be obedient to the command of Jesus that he knew from John's Gospel 'to love one another'. He was, for both Ninian and Patrick, the father of faith.

Ninian and Patrick created the distinctive pattern of Christian communities which, a century later, were the most significant feature of the Christian Church in Britain. Communities were founded on the Irish pattern in Cumbria by St. Mungo, known as Kentigern in the local language. In 553, Mungo was fleeing persecution from Strathclyde and journeying to north Wales to join Christians living in community. As he journeyed through Rheged, he met a prince of the kingdom who begged him to stay and bring the faith to his kingdom. Mungo told him that he had a vision of founding a new community in a place where two lakes met, overshadowed by mountains. The following day, Mungo came to a clearing between the Derwentwater and Bassenthwaite lakes and immediately recognised the site of his new community, and there he set up his cross—the place now bears that name, Crosthwaite. Here, he became known as 'The Hound Lord' in the local language, or Kentigern; perhaps this relates to him being the leader of his community.

The communities of Ninian, Patrick and Kentigern all followed a similar pattern. They were basically Anglo-Saxon stockade settlements built on or nearby rivers or lakes. The round Anglo-Saxon houses provided communal living for families and individuals. Like modern day Coptic religions, the only indication that any individual was a monk, nun, priest or bishop was in the style of clothing and a shaven forehead. The distinctive feature of the Christian communities was the central building which served as church, scriptorium or school, as well as infirmary or guest house. This building was always aligned east to west, and the church only had one small window, high in the east gable end. The members of the community waited patiently in darkness every Sunday morning for the first light of dawn to appear through the east window, to signal the start of the Eucharist. This model of community was remarkably successful, increasing the population of Ireland dramatically from the end of the fifth century and life expectancy. Whilst Kentigern's community at Crosthwaite is the only known site dating from the sixth century, it seems likely that there would have been others. Most likely is Urswick in Furness which at the time would have been sited at the top of a river estuary, and there is a very good archaeological case to be made for it being an ancient site.

Christian Cumbria

The story of established Christian communities, though, doesn't begin until the beginning of the seventh century. Edwin, who killed Aethelfrith of Bernicia with the support of Eadbald—the Christian king of Kent—married Aethelburg, a Kentish princess, and so converted to Christianity. At this time, though, the kingdom of Rheged, and much of modern Cumbria, was not under the control of Edwin as king of Northumbria. Edwin was killed in 630, and Northumbria reverted back to paganism. In

632, the middle of Aethelfrith's three sons, Oswald, came to challenge for his father's throne. Oswald had been exiled after his father's death and was taken in by the community of Iona. Oswald, together with his younger brother Oswy and sister Ebba, had been brought up by the community of St. Columba. Although Columba himself died in 597 and Oswald wasn't born until 601, his influence must have been great on the young family. The rule of Columcille (Columba's Gaelic name) became widespread, being used in communities across Britain until the tenth century. Its five hundred or more sayings, 'rules' in terms of living a holy life, were very simple: 'Wisdom without learning is to be preferred to learning without wisdom'.[4] Oswald became the iconic pattern for kingship in the world of dark-age monarchy. Charlemagne, a century later, regarded him to be the ultimate role model and dedicated chapels to him across the Carolingian empire. Alfred the Great, inspired by the stories of his bravery and wisdom, made him personal patron saint. Most importantly, for us, it is through Oswald that Cumbria can be spoken of for the first time as a Christian county.

During the ten years of Oswald's reign, Northumbria expanded to become the dominating kingdom of Britain. Oswald was named as *braetwalda* which means 'the king of all kings' in Britain, all paid homage to him, and his rule was law. Oswald championed Christianity for all the benefits that it brought his people, not least a personal faith in Jesus Christ. Oswald was an evangelist himself, often preaching and exhorting his people to believe in Jesus. He was accompanied on many occasions by Aidan, for whom Oswald acted as interpreter. Oswald, through alliance, marriage of his relatives and his victories in war,

---

[4] Excerpts from the *Rule of St. Columcille* are included in collections of writing entitled 'The Alphabet of Devotion'.

Growing Spirituality

forged Northumbria into a kingdom that stretched from Chester to Edinburgh, controlling most of northern England and southern Scotland. Cumbria was therefore in the heartland of his kingdom, and the number of churches dedicated to him betrays the origins of Christianity in the county. Although only monarch from 632 to 642, his influence has proved to be immense. In many ways, 642 is the key date in the faith history of Cumbria; in this date, Cumbria becomes a Christian land, and the church becomes the essential focus of community life.

The founding of Christian Cumbria, though, is not just the story of one person. It is the tale of many individuals expressing their faith with great courage and patience. It is the story of Aidan, Hilda, Cuthbert, Herbert, Bega and Bede. Each played their part in building on the foundations laid by Ninian, Patrick and Kentigern. Often described as the 'Golden Age of Northumbria', the stories of their faith and the things they accomplished can inspire Christians afresh to overcome difficulties and divisions to become Christ's faithful disciples in our modern church.

So what was the life of faith that someone like Aidan lived? He stood firmly in the tradition of Christian communities first known at Whithorn. Lindisfarne[5] was modelled on Iona; the daily routine of prayer was central, together with the ministry of welcome and hospitality, as well as the school and copying of ancient manuscripts. Aidan also followed Columcille's example by walking thousands of miles, meeting people and converting or encouraging them in the faith. It was said, though, of Aidan that he never pressed the faith upon another person; when he met someone, he would ask them if they knew of Jesus. If not, he questioned whether they would like to know; if they declined,

---

[5] *Lindis* means 'land', and *farne* is 'island', so the name very aptly means 'land-island'.

it was said he would simply bless them and move on. Such a generous open heart was remarkable, even in the seventh century. Many, though, did wish to know of Jesus and were nurtured by the milk of his simple teaching.

Aidan was passionate, though, about justice and caring for the poor. All the gifts and donations given to the community at Lindisfarne were devoted to buying children out of slavery. Those who were saved were brought with the royal children to be taught in the community school. So Chad and Cedd, who were saved by Aidan from slavery, were taught alongside Hilda, the royal princess. The teaching they received was among the finest available. Aldhelm, a Saxon prince, writes of the education he received at Lindisfarne in the tradition of Aidan at the beginning of the eighth century, in which he 'described the thorough grounding in grammar, mathematics, physics and exegesis that was taught by them'[6]. Aidan, though, was not acquisitive at all, even for those he might save; the stories of Aidan depict a man who was selfless, not only of his own property but of others as well. In Aidan's old age, King Oswin became worried about Aidan's failing health and so provided him with a horse, only for the saint to give it to the first poor man he met. As a result of Aidan's persistent generosity, the king eventually supplied him with a horse to ride and a supply of horses to give to those whom he met.

Aidan, though, lived in violent times. Oswald constantly had to defend his kingdom and its citizens from the attacks of raiders from Mercia. After his friend's death, Oswy and Oswin jointly ruled the kingdom, but the uncle and nephew didn't work well together. Aidan, for over nine years, tried to bring them

---

[6] *Early Celtic Christianity* by Brendan Lehane, Constable, London, 1994 (p.145).

Growing Spirituality

together, but in vain, Oswy had his nephew murdered just a few days before Aidan himself died in 651. Bede writes most warmly of Aidan, and his words are those of affectionate remembrance: 'Such were his love of peace and charity, temperance and humility; his soul which triumphed over anger and greed and at the same time despised pride and vainglory; his industry in carrying out and teaching the divine commandments and his tenderness in comforting the weak, relieving and protecting the poor'.[7]

Hilda was a contemporary of Oswald, Aidan and Cuthbert. She was probably even a relative of Oswald and Cuthbert; certainly, she was a member of the royal family. It is a sign of the very different attitudes to the role of women in Anglo-Saxon society that Hilda is still well known and celebrated. Four centuries later, women would never have been allowed to be on equal terms with archbishops and monarchs, and yet Hilda was regarded as superior to them all.

Hilda was born at the beginning of the seventh century in around 618. Hereswitha, her sister, married Aethelric, king of the East Angles, and both sisters were known for their personal devotion as children being taught by St. Aidan. Hereswitha helped to found a community at Chelles in Gaul, and there appears to be a link between the sisters and the church in France; it may be that both of them travelled to Gaul at different times. Certainly, it was Hilda's intention to go and found a community in Gaul when Bede tells us she met Aidan, who persuaded her to stay in Northumbria and to found a community. By tradition, she established her double house at the place where she met Aidan,

---

[7] *The Ecclesiastical History of the English People* by Bede (book 3, chapter 17).

on the cliffs at Whitby. It was not unknown for a woman to take the role of abbot for one or more communities; St. Ita at Killeedy in Limerick presided in exactly the same way over a double house. Hilda was trained under the Rule of Columcille which appears to have made no distinction between men and women in terms of leadership. Indeed, the Irish communities are full of examples of feisty women from the time of St. Brigid onwards. Hilda, though, was no hangover from the church's Irish heritage. She was regarded by the Roman scholar Eddius as 'a very wise woman, the best of comforters and counselors in the whole province'[8]. The words of St. Wilfrid's biographer, praising this Celtic princess brought up according to Columcille's Rule, begins to give the lie to the supposed great division of the church at the Synod of Whitby in 664.

Eddius, in his words, gives the clue as to why it had to be Hilda in the chair at Whitby. It may have not been unusual to have a woman in the role of abbot, even in a double community. What was unusual was that for the first time in Britain, she led a specialist community; Whitby was a theological school for men and women. The monks and nuns didn't work the land; they didn't look after the animals or bring in the crops. Their role was purely education and study. Hilda presided over the first theological colleges in Britain. So wealthy were the two houses that they were run by paid staff. Hilda was not simply a woman acting in the role of abbot; she was also the wisest teacher and most effective business manager. So why didn't the Archbishop of Canterbury chair the synod? Why wasn't the synod in Canterbury? Of course, the synod was called to deal with a particular problem for the king and queen of Northumbria, but church leaders came from far and wide to join the discussions. It

---

[8] *Early Celtic Christianity* by Brendan Lehane, Constable, London, 1994 (p. 202).

was a debate for the whole of the church in Britain. Colman came from Innisboffin, Donegal. Agilbert was from Gaul and was Bishop of the West Saxons, Romanus came from Ely, representing the churches in the kingdoms of the Angles, and of course, there was the local talent—Wilfrid, Chad and, supremely, Cuthbert.

Archbishop Frithuwine[9] was the sixth person to hold the See at Canterbury. He had become Archbishop in 655 and so would have been well known to Queen Eanflaed as she came from Kent. It wouldn't have been surprising if he was then asked to preside at the synod, so why wasn't he? The answer is simple: among all these pious and charismatic leaders of the church at that time, Hilda's spirituality stood far above the rest. Bede says of her: 'All who knew Hilda, the handmaiden of Christ and abbess, used to call her mother because of her outstanding devotion and grace'.[10] She died in 680 after a long illness of six years, during which she was in great pain, but she was greatly mourned by all who knew her, and Bede gives her the final epitaph as being 'the light of Britain' and concluded, 'Her life was an example of works of light, blessed not only to herself but to many who desired to live uprightly'.[11]

Although there is no record of Hilda visiting Cumbria, the role of a woman playing such a significant part in the most important Synod of the seventh century would have had an impact. She

---

[9] There is some debate as to the Archbishop's name; possible alternatives are Deusdedit or Frithona.
[10] *The Ecclesiastical History of the English People* by Bede (book 4, chapter 23).
[11] *The Ecclesiastical History of the English People* by Bede (book 4, chapter 23).

was a woman who trained five of the first bishops of the national Church of England—Bosa, Aetla, Oftfor, John and Wilfrid, as well as numerous abbots and abbesses. Her role in establishing the finest teaching in the Christian communities cannot be overstated. The Christian communities would have benefited directly from her influence and indirectly through the charismatic visits of Cuthbert.

Cuthbert, friend to Cumbria
It is believed that Cuthbert was born in 634, and although there are several stories of him as a child, it is Aidan's death that propels him into the limelight. In 651, Cuthbert was on Doddington Moor, overlooking the Northumbria coast, when he saw a vision of light streaming from Bamburgh up into heaven, and as he watched, he saw the soul of a holy man being borne on angel's wings. Cuthbert responded to this vision by getting on his horse and riding to Melrose. What is strange about this is that there are several communities closer in 651, most notably Lindisfarne. Of course, the fact that at seventeen, he had a horse to ride and was free to roam around, suggests that he was a warrior of the king's army, as well as a prince.

Cuthbert arrived the following day at Melrose, and as he came to the gate of the community, he gave all his possessions, including his horse, to the poor begging at the gate. The prior Boisil saw him approaching and said, 'Behold the servant of the Lord'. Cuthbert, from this moment on, became the most spiritual charismatic Christian in life (until 687) and in death for the generations that have followed. Boisil was Cuthbert's mentor, and from him, he learnt the Rule of Columcille and the monk's way of life. Cuthbert excelled in everything he did, but from the first, he was recognised for the great gift of healing. Bede says of him that healing came through prayer whether Cuthbert was present with the sick person or not. People flocked to him at

Melrose and then with Wilfrid at Ripon to receive his healing touch and to ask prayers on behalf of their loved ones. The seventh century was the time of repeated outbreaks of plague. Melrose was not immune, and Cuthbert himself was struck down; he had a vision to show that he would recover but that Boisil wouldn't. So it turned out that Cuthbert became prior in Boisil's place in 661.

Cuthbert's influence at the Synod of Whitby was immense. Although he is not reported as speaking in the debate, it was Cuthbert who encouraged the various communities to adopt the dating of Easter, and he himself adopted the tonsure which encouraged many others to do likewise. Cuthbert travelled vast distances, encouraging the communities in all the lands of the Northumbria over lordship, as well as visiting many solitaries, including his friend, St. Herebert, on an island in Derwentwater. Bede writes especially of his love for those living in the most remote areas: 'Cuthbert frequently went forth from the monastery, sometimes on horseback but more often on foot; he came to the neighbouring villages and preached the way of truth, just as Boisil had been accustomed to do in his time. Now, it was the custom amongst the English people at that time, when a clerk or priest came to the village, for all to gather at his command to hear the Word, gladly listening to what was said. So great was Cuthbert's eloquence, so keen his desire to drive home what he had begun to teach, so bright the light of his angelic countenance, that none of those present would presume to hide from him the secrets of their hearts. Now, he used especially to make for those places and preach in those villages that were far away on steep and rugged mountains which others dreaded to visit and whose poverty and ignorance kept other teachers away. Giving himself up gladly to this devoted labour, he attended to their instruction with such industry that he would leave the monastery and often not return home for a whole week and even occasionally for a whole month; but he would linger among the hill folk, calling the peasants to heavenly things both by the words he said and by his virtuous deeds'.[12] Bede gives no clue where these hill folk lived, but many must have been among the fells of Cumbria.

It seemed at first that Cuthbert adopted the prayer practice of Ninian, Dewi and Columcille of praying alone in or by the sea. Visiting Ebba's[13] community of Coldingham, Cuthbert was observed slipping out in the night and walking into the North Sea with outstretched arms as the waves came up to his neck. Cuthbert prayed silently, and as he did, sea otters came nuzzling against his body to keep him warm. It appears from his earliest days in the community at Melrose that the hermit's life became increasingly attractive to him, yet he could get no space or solitude from all those who sought his healing touch, wisdom and prayer.

Becoming the abbot of Lindisfarne, he sought the solitude he craved, and he would withdraw from the community onto the opposite small island that now bears his name, often standing in the small channel and allowing the waves to cover his body as the tide came in whilst he stood in pray. Even this solitude was denied to him, as people would swim the channel to come and see him. So Cuthbert then determined to build a cell on the Inner Farne, still within sight of Lindisfarne and Bamburgh but no longer accessible to the causal swimmer! He built his cell on the pattern of St. Antony of Egypt. Here, he enjoyed peace; at least,

---

[12] The story as told by Bede in Book 4, Chapter 27 of *The Ecclesiastical History of the English People*, translated by Bertram Colgrave, Oxford World's Classics, OUP, 2008.

[13] Ebba was the sister of St. Oswald and Oswy.

Growing Spirituality

once he had sorted out the local wildlife. It is told that he planted a garden, but as soon as he had finished, the sea birds came and ate all the seed. So Cuthbert called all the animals to him and proposed that he should draw a line down the middle of the garden, and everything on the left, he would leave for them to eat, and everything on the right was his, a solution that worked well thereafter.

In 685, this most charismatic character was elected bishop, much to his own reluctance. As ever, though, he entered into his new role in the style of Aidan, being a peripatetic teacher, encourager and healer, but after only two years, he returned to Lindisfarne, exhausted. Before returning, though, he made one last visit to his old friend, St. Herbert, on Derwentwater, on which occasion Bede tells us, 'Cuthbert said, "Brother Herebert, I am certain that the time of my departure and of laying aside my earthly tabernacle is at hand". When Herebert heard this, he said with tears, "I beseech you by the Lord not to desert me but to remember your most faithful companion and ask the merciful Lord that, as we served Him together on earth, we may journey together to the skies to behold His grace in heaven". The bishop gave himself up to prayer and forthwith, having learnt in spirit that he gained what he sought from the Lord, he said, "Do not weep but be glad because the Lord in His mercy has granted what we asked of Him". The issue of events confirmed the truth of the prophecy, for after they had separated, they did not see each other in the flesh, but their spirits left their bodies on one and the same day'.[14]

---

[14] The story as told by Bede in Book 4, Chapter 29 of *The Ecclesiastical History of the English People*, translated by Bertram Colgrave, Oxford World's Classics, OUP, 2008.

Cuthbert was a celebrity in life and remains the most attractive of all the Celtic saints, even to this day. Bede wrote of him, 'He taught them what should be done but first showed them how to do it by his own example. He was before all things fired with divine love'.[15]

Many of those who founded the church in the seventh century are forgotten, and many are overlooked. How many people know of Bega, after whom St. Bees is named and whose bracelet, for so many years, was part of Cumberland's crest? Bega herself is little known to the modern Christians, yet her story is bound with the history of the seventh-century church and the development of Christianity in Cumbria. She, like so many others, seems to have been a royal princess. Her story tells of a desire to found a community after the example of St. Ita near Waterford. Her father, though, had other ideas and betrothed her to an Irish prince, probably a relative of the Uí Néills. This seems likely, given that she arrived in Cumbria from Ulster when she made her flight from her unwanted suitor. Bega set about building her community in around 650 and attracting to her those who would share in the common life. There are so few historical details that many writers place her life much later in the ninth century or even consider her mythological. However, it is certain that Bega was a real person, as she appears in the Annals of Ulster, and there are other mentions of her name in various forms well before the fourteenth century *Life of St. Bega* appeared.

Bega fits more properly into the time of Cuthbert and Hilda. All the more so because, like Cuthbert, she sought the peace of the life of prayer in being a solitary. Bega, having seen the

---

[15] *The Ecclesiastical History of the English People* by Bede (book 4, chapter 28).

Growing Spirituality

community established and seeking a way to avoid the attention caused by her bracelet's healing miracles, tried to find a place to be wholly devoted to prayer. Like Cuthbert, she looked for a thin place near water. However, there were no convenient islands near St. Bees Bay, so she travelled almost certainly deliberately to be near Kentigern's cross and built her cell nearby. It may have been that by the mid-seventh century, Crosthwaite was already a place of pilgrimage, and so it would be natural for Bega herself to be near but not too close to the shore of Lake Bassenthwaite. Her death is not recorded, but as a high cross was set up next to her cell and as it became a place of pilgrimage, it would seem likely that the site of the present church is where Bega died.

End of the Golden Age
The Golden Age of the founding Christians of Cumbria came to an end with the death of the Venerable Bede in 735. By the end of the eighth century, the first attacks of the Norsemen had been made on Lindisfarne. By the end of the ninth century, the coastal Christian communities had been abandoned, and the north of England and parts of Scotland and Ireland had been colonised by the Vikings. Although converting to Christianity immediately, a greater change was coming upon the county and its churches. The end of the Anglo-Saxon and Danish kingdom and society of the tenth century would suddenly be destroyed, but the faith of the founding saints would live on.

The final words of Bede's most famous work, *The Ecclesiastical History of the English People*, are perhaps the best epitaph of the time from Ninian to Bede which saw Christianity firmly established in Cumbria: 'In these favourable times of peace and prosperity, many of the Northumbrian race, both noble and simple, have laid aside their weapons and taken the tonsure, preferring that they and their children should take monastic vows rather than train themselves in the art of war. Let the earth rejoice in the Lord's perpetual kingdom and let Britain rejoice in His faith and let the multitude of isles be glad and give thanks at the remembrance of His holiness'.[16]

---

[16] *The Ecclesiastical History of the English People* by Bede (book 5, chapter 24).

Chapter Three
A place of prayer

The trouble with history is that it can be too familiar. The year 1066 is perhaps the best known date in English history. The significance of the year for generations of school children is that it marks the beginning of our history. How sad that such a tragic event is regarded as a beginning! The fact that 1066 is so well known, though, does pay tribute to the skillful lies told by the Norman historians.

A century of suffering

In Cumbria's history, it is the winter of 1069–1070 that is the most significant date, rather than the Battle of Hastings three years earlier. The events of that winter bring a dreadful close to the Anglo-Saxon and Norse history that had shaped the north from the fifth century onwards. 'The harrying of the north' is altogether too understated a title for the savagery unleashed by King William upon those who opposed him. In the space of six months, it is believed that nearly 40 percent of the population of Cumbria died. No one, though, can be sure of the numbers. The systematic murder of men, women and children and the destruction of whole villages, as well as stocks of winter food, caused the devastation of the whole of the north. Orderic Vitalis wrote about the events, saying:

'The King stopped at nothing to hunt his enemies. He cut down many people and destroyed homes and land. Nowhere else had he shown such cruelty. To his shame the King made no effort to control his fury, punishing the innocent with the guilty. He

*ordered that crops and herds, tools and food be burned to ashes.
More than 100,000 people perished of starvation'.*[17]

So great was the loss of life and the destruction of the social
fabric that the Domesday book in 1086 records hundreds of
villages deserted. In addition, all local leadership was removed.
Of the eighteen hundred thanes named in the Anglo-Saxon
Chronicle in 1065, only two were recorded in the Domesday
Book. This represents an unparalleled removal of the Anglo-
Saxon and Norse leadership that, since 937, had created a
prosperous and creative society. The church did not fare any
better under the conquest, with Edward the Confessor's
Archbishop Stigand dying in mysterious circumstances in the
winter of 1069. He was immediately replaced by the Norman
Abbot of Caen, Lanfranc. Little trace remains of the vibrant
Anglo-Saxon and Norse churches in Cumbria. Their buildings
were systematically destroyed, and the stonework used as rubble
for the new Norman churches. A clear example is Ireby Old
Church which has, in the outer walls, Anglo-Saxon stonework
and carvings from an unknown church. Indeed, there are few
Norman buildings where the stones from the previous churches
are not reused in some way.

The period of English history from 1066 to 1154 is a story of
violence and destruction. One of the conqueror's sons probably
killed his brother to become king. His granddaughter and
grandnephew waged a cruel civil war that impoverished the
nation. Only in 1154, with the agreement of the contesting
parties to the accession of Henry II, did anything resembling the
pre-conquest society begin to re-emerge. It is significant,
therefore, that many of the religious foundations of Cumbria

---

[17] *The Ecclesiastical History of England and Normandy* by
Vitalis (p. 28).

date from the fifty years after Henry II's accession. Quite simply, the wanton destruction of the winter of 1069 wrecked the social fabric of Cumbria. This included the Christian communities which were the heartbeat of the church. Cumbria became a lawless depopulated frontier region which laid the foundations for the English and Scottish Reivers, whose activities plagued the borderland until 1603.

The 'harrying of the north' was not the only impact the Norman Conquest had on the churches of Cumbria. Farther away in Rome, the Normans also brought their malevolent influence upon the whole church. Prior to 1049, the Bishop of Rome had simply been known as 'the Vicar of St. Peter's tomb'. The Bishop of Rome was a spiritual guide and leader in the church, whose influence was due to the understanding of pilgrimage to the tomb of St. Peter. From 1049, this changed dramatically; Leo IX was 'elected' Pope under threats from the Duke of Normandy in political alliance with the Holy Roman Emperor. In the eleventh century, the Normans were the dominant political and military force of Western Europe. Leo IX laid the foundations for the expansionist papacy of his successor Gregory VII. During his time, the Papal State was established, along with an army of mercenaries. The Pope assumed the altogether grander title of 'The Vicar of Christ' and claimed authority to be the sole appointee of all senior clergy. This effectively gave the Pope control of the church. The Eastern empire, not being dominated by the same political concerns, broke with the West in 1080 under the guise of a point of doctrine in the Nicene Creed but, more pragmatically, due to a rejection of this new expansionist papacy. Richard Southern in his classic history of the Middle Ages states with irony:

'There are no words which convey the spirit of the medieval papacy so brilliantly as the trenchant statements of the papal

*position inserted in Gregory VII's letters. Among these
statements we find the following: the pope can be judged by no
one; the pope alone can depose and restore bishops; he alone
can make new ecclesial laws; all princes should kiss his feet; an
appeal to the papal court inhibits judgement by all inferior
courts; and, a pope is made a saint by the merits of St. Peter'.*[18]

For Cumbria, the new expansionist papacy brought huge
changes for the parochial ministry. In the twelfth century, as the
church became re-established under Henry II, the style and
leadership was radically different from that of the previous
Anglo-Saxon and Norse parishes. For example, all clergy,
monks and nuns were required to be celibate. Anyone who has
read Ellis Peter's novel, *The Potter's Field,* will have read of
the entirely accurate description of the potter being forced to
reject his wife, make her destitute and give his land to
Shrewsbury Abbey in order to join the community. This church
is very different from St. Hilda's mixed community at Whitby
in the seventh century. The thirteenth century, though, saw a
religious revival with twenty-six pre-Reformation monastic
houses being founded in Cumbria. The style of these
communities, though, was very different from those of St.
Columba and his successors. Governed by a lord abbot, these
houses were major landowners supplying funds to the papacy
and support for the Lord Bishop in Rose Castle. The Bishop of
Carlisle, like the Pope, had his own army, on several occasions
even leading his troops personally into battle. This was a very
different style of bishop to St. Cuthbert six centuries earlier.

Given the destruction of the social fabric between 1069 and
1154, the crown had assumed control of Cumbria, along with

---

[18] *Western Society and the Church in the Middle Ages* by R. W.
Southern, Penguin, London, 1970 (p. 102).

Growing Spirituality

the Norman lords who were given huge tracts as part of the conquest's settlement. An example of this is the Le Fleming family, who later build Rydal Hall. They were given large estates at Aldingham, Beckermet, Coniston, Dalton, Gleaston, Seascale and Urswick. These estates were in addition to their holdings in other parts of England. The Le Fleming family claimed descendence from the first Earl of Flanders, Baldwin, and his successor, another Baldwin, was King William's father-in-law in 1066 and one of the five thousand knights to fight for the Duke at Hastings. During the thirteenth century, Sir John le Fleming, like many other Norman lords, 'took the cross' to fight in the crusades and, as a sign of his devotion, gave land and money to found a monastic house. Ann Galbraith, in her book on the Fleming family records, says,

'Sir John le Fleming of Beckermet, Knight gave the patronage of the Rectory of Arlecden and the land in Great Beckermet to the Abby of Chaldine, (Calder Abbey) in the twenty-sixth year of King Henry III (1242)'.[19]

Twenty-six monastic houses are recorded as being founded in Cumbria after 1066 and being still in operation at the time of the Dissolution in 1538. The first house was the Augustinian foundation which is now Carlisle Cathedral. In 1092, William II re-founded Carlisle, and in 1133, Henry I created the diocese with Athelwold as its first bishop in a castle made from rose-coloured sandstone. Bishop Athelwold was given vast lands in Cumbria and was a prince bishop. His appointment was political, and on several occasions, he fought the Scottish kings to keep the city and the diocese under England's control. Athelwold, as a former prior of an Augustinian house, created a

---

[19] *The Fleming Family of Rydal Hall* by Ann Galbraith (privately published in 2010).

foundation within the new city walls of Carlisle. Under the influence of the Augustinians at Carlisle, many of the new monastic houses of the thirteenth century followed an Augustinian rule, most famously at Lanercost. Whist fifteen foundations were Augustinian, the remaining eleven were part of the reformed Benedictine order, and of these, the Savignac house at Furness became the most influential.

Augustinians in Cumbria

The rule of St. Augustine of Hippo dates from around the year 400. It was popularised by the Norman influence across Western Europe in the eleventh century. Part of the reason for this was disillusionment with the Rule of St. Benedict in the European monastic houses (communities in Cumbria, up until this time, continued to use the very different Rule of St. Columcille). The growth of towns, increasing literacy and more stable forms of regional government meant that many sought a more detached form of Christian community not tainted by the world. Allied to this was the shock to medieval Europe of the attack on Jerusalem and the Islamic control of Christian holy sites which gave rise to the Crusades. Although Christian pilgrims were not prevented from visiting the Holy Land and Christianity was respected by the Muslim overlords, the Pope gave instructions to the princes of Europe to fight a holy war. This atmosphere of increased personal devotion to 'take the cross' is difficult for the modern mind to understand, but it was a powerful influence in creating the prayer houses of Cumbria. As well as obviously being the rule for Augustinians, in 1059, at the Lateran Council, 'The Rule of St. Augustine' was approved for the use of all clergy. Of significance for Cumbria, it was also the rule chosen for the Cistercian, Dominican, Gilbertine and Premonstratensian abbeys.

Augustine's rule is quite short and gives an outline of the religious life. It lays down governance covering detachment, acts of charity, community prayers, fasting, care of the infirmed, schooling and silence, as well as observing the three principles of chastity, poverty and obedience. It is also collegiate in style, and therefore, the order is understood as a fraternity.

Augustine's rule, though, being so short and not being detailed, allowed for a great deal of flexibility in its implementation. In Cumbria, at first, these houses were noted for their simple lifestyle and devotion. Often, the houses would divide the brothers between those who were dedicated entirely to prayer and contemplation and those who were working brothers. Both groups attended the seven offices of the day, but those working in the kitchen, infirmary, school or on the estate were busy keeping the monastery functioning. The other brothers would dedicate themselves entirely to silence, prayer and reflection. In the thirteenth century, there was no division of status between the two groups. Later on, as the houses became extremely wealthy, the temptation grew to live a lavish lifestyle, for the abbot to assume the role of the local lord, and for the working brothers to be of lower status. The ruins of many of their abbeys demonstrate this division of status, wealth and power. Even a causal visitor cannot help to wonder at the difference between the accommodation for the abbot or prior and those brothers working in the kitchens. A typical example is the prior's tower at Lanercost, this magnificent four-story building being converted by Lord Dacre for his own lavish home in the sixteenth century.

The Augustinian legacy to Cumbria, though, should not be underestimated. They didn't bring contemplative prayer to the county, nor was their rule of life the first discipline of Christian communities in this part of England. However, coming after the chaos and destruction of the previous hundred years, the Augustinians did make this county a place of prayer for the next three hundred years. Visiting the sites of their abbeys today, it is striking that they chose places of remarkable stillness and peace. The location of their abbeys, though chosen for many reasons, illustrates the centrality of detachment and silence in the Augustinian rule. Though their influence was lost in Cumbria at the time of the dissolution of the monasteries, the Augustinian rule continues to offer this way of silence in contemplative prayer.

Martin Laird is perhaps the best known of contemporary Augustinian writers. In his classic book, *Into the Silent Land*, Laird explores the necessity of silence to the life of prayer. The beginning of his book is a manifesto for silent prayer:

'We are built for contemplation. Communion with God in the silence of the heart is a God-given capacity, like the rhododendron's capacity to flower, the fledgling's for flight and the child's for self-forgetful abandon and joy'.[20]

For Augustinians then, silent prayer was not about technique and a style of praying. Rather, silence was 'the homeland of the soul'. To have such a rich Augustinian heritage both in the diocesan cathedral and in the sites of so many pre-Reformation abbeys speaks to us still of their priority of prayer, a priority which, in their understanding, springs from our essential God-given nature rather something that we adopt or copy for ourselves.

Martin Laird describes the essential nature of the Augustinian's understanding of prayer, when he writes,

---

[20] *Into the Silent Land* by Martin Laird, DLT, London, 2006 (p. 1).

'There are two contemplative practices of fundamental importance in the Christian tradition: the practice of stillness (also called meditation, still prayer, contemplative prayer) and the practice of watchfulness or awareness.[21]

For Laird, 'God is our homeland' and these two practices of prayer are typical of the Augustinian detachment from the world as the soul 'rests' in God. Stillness and watchfulness are the keys to Augustinian prayer. These twin practices are not understood as a route to find God; rather, they are the experience of being with God. This is a world view that the Lord Bishop Athelwold and the first monks at Carlisle would have known and understood when he says,

'An ancient Christian view is that the foundation of every land is silence, where God simply and perpetually gives Himself. This self-gift is manifested in the creation, in the people of God and their inspired (if stumbling) pursuit of a just society, and most fully, in the Christian view of things, in Jesus Christ. This is the homeland, to which every spiritual pilgrim is constantly being called, called home, as St. Augustine says, "from the noise that is around us to the joys that are silent. Why do we rush about looking for God who is here at home with us, if all we want is to be with him"'.[22]

The Rule of Benedict
Important though the Augustinians were for our common story of faith in Cumbria, their rule and practice are not the only reasons why this county became such a vibrant place of prayer. The Christian journey in North West England in the pre-

---

[21] Ibid., 5.
[22] Ibid., 6.

Reformation centuries is also the story of the Benedictines. Whilst the majority of houses founded in the thirteenth century are Augustinian, there are also nearly as many Benedictine. The significant absence from the religious life in Cumbria, of course, is the lack of any Franciscans; this is ironic, given the strength of the Tertiary Franciscans in the contemporary church. Carmelites also were absent apart from the Whitefriars at Appleby. Often, the foundations of the abbeys were related to the expectations and experience of those lords and their ladies who gave grants of lands and gifts. These were connected with praying for the souls of the departed, together with hospitality experienced on their travels. So it seems that the Norman elite in Cumbria were content to keep to their preference for Augustinians, although there were some who were more inclined towards the practical and worldly rule of Benedict, especially under the influence of their travels for the crusades. Interestingly, the foundation at Appleby of a Carmelite order in 1281 was a result of a gift of the Percy family from the North East. It seems likely that the self-denying friars' intent on serving the needs of the poor was more in keeping with Lord Percy's own faith.

Benedict's rule is altogether a more complete pattern than Augustine's. Born fifty years after St. Augustine's death, Benedict lived in a very different world. Esther de Waal calls it 'a world without landmarks'. Certainly, it was a world in turmoil; the great power of Rome had fallen, and barbarian tribes were ransacking much of the old empire. The church itself was riven with dispute and arguments. Benedict looked back to St. Antony of Egypt who lived nearly two centuries earlier. He looked back to a time when Christianity was rooted in contemplative prayer, in the deserts where the pilgrim was welcomed, and where the scriptures were the inspiration for the faithful. In Benedict's time, the scriptures themselves had become the pawns of political and theological dispute. De Waal notes the humanity of Benedict's rule and how it seems to embody his own personality. She says of his words:

'This is the work of a man who has lived what he is writing about, both in the cave at Subiaco and in the monastic enclosure at Monte Cassino. The consummate wisdom which it shows could have emerged from a long and through assimilation, not simply in his mind but in his whole being'.[23]

Perhaps because of his own experience, his rule expresses the two great hallmarks of the Benedictines: 'hospitality' and 'welcoming Christ'. All strangers and pilgrims were to be treated in the same way as Christ entering the house. Quoting St. Matthew's Gospel, Benedict saw the parable of the sheep and goats as being a literal truth: 'I was a stranger and you welcomed me'. The Benedictine rule indeed roots itself in scripture, the practice of 'holy reading' (Lectio Divina) being originally a Benedictine practice. The importance of prayerfully being soaked in the Bible and resting in silence to hear God's word is a uniquely Benedictine practice. Father Cyprian Smith from the Benedictine Monastery at Appleforth comments on this important aspect of Benedict's teaching:

'We are reminded that The Rule of St. Benedict begins with the word, 'listen'. Properly understood, this is the key to his whole teaching. A monk should be above all a listener. So indeed should every Christian. The whole spiritual life of a Christian is a process of listening to God, inclining the ear of the heart. This image of the inward ear, the ear of the heart, shows us that our listening is not merely an intellectual or rational activity, it is

---

[23] *Seeking God* by Esther de Waal, Canterbury Press, Norwich, 1999 (p. 5).

intuitive, springing from the very core of our being; where we are most open to God, most receptive to the word he speaks'.[24]

As with Augustine, the rule requires three fundamental vows. Yet here, too, Benedict shows his humanity; for him, these are virtues to which members of his community are called to return to over and over again. They are not the harsh detachment from the ordinary affections and life of the world. Rather, the rule of Benedict is based on three principles which, at their heart, are not world-denying, but rather, for the building-up of the individual's relationship with God. Obedience is the first; this vow is about the fundamental relationship with God. Benedict understands God to be love; therefore, it is an obedience to be loved. Obedience is not therefore to be understood to be adhering to the authority of the abbot, master or even God. Rather, it is the gift of the free will to ascend into the love of the Father. It is also obedience to the community to recognise that those who are also loved by God are our brothers and sisters. De Waal recognises this as being fundamental to the rule:

'It is the new understanding of the relationships between the members of the community that is the great breakthrough. The older ideal had been essentially that of a novice finding a holy man and asking to learn from him, and the monastery had been a group of individuals gathered round the feet of a sage. One of these earlier rules, 'The Rule of the Master' had given enormous power to the abbot. St. Benedict changes this almost exclusively vertical pattern of authority by emphasising the relationships of the monks with each other. They are of course disciples who

---

[24] *The Path of Life* by Cyprian Smith, OSB, Gracewing, 1996 (pp. 6–7).

Growing Spirituality

have come to the monastery to be trained, but they are also brothers bound in love to each other'.[25]

Second is the vow of stability. Benedictines, unlike other religious orders, join a community rather than the order itself. This means there is commitment to be in a loving fellowship with one another. In 2012, I attended Vespers at Ampleforth. The abbot explained that this was the one office that continued in Latin when the others had been changed to English. What was the reason for this? 'In order', explained the abbot, 'that the departed brothers could still join in with the present community in prayer'. That could only happen in a Benedictine house. This vow of stability demonstrates a realistic understanding that the way of a Christian can be hard. Difficulties are not to be avoided; rather, they are to be faced, worked through and overcome. It is important to note that Benedict gives a great deal of teaching on this subject. His 'twelve steps of humility' describe an inward conversion of the heart that leads to a change in our outward behaviour. His teaching, as ever, is rooted in scripture, in the example of Jesus from the Gospels. He advises that as we get closer to Christ in our relationship of prayer, the greater the divine presence, and the more dignity is given to our littleness.

Thirdly, there is the vow which is difficult to translate into English. 'Conversatio morum' is a Latin expression which means 'conversation of life' but is perhaps better translated as 'faithfully living'. This is much more than chastity and poverty, for unlike many other rules and especially Augustine's, this is not detachment from the world, but rather, embracing life. It is about being open to the world but remaining faithful and being willing to follow where Christ leads. 'We believe that the divine

---

[25] De Waal, op. cit., 4.

presence is everywhere', comments St. Benedict, 'we should believe this all the more, without any doubt whatsoever, when we attend to the divine work'.[26]

The Benedictine houses of the thirteenth to sixteenth centuries in Cumbria were places of prayer. The context, though, of prayer was different from that of their Augustinian brothers and sisters. Whilst we recognise this common root of contemplative prayer, the forgoing discussion of what is distinctive to each of these great spiritual traditions is helpful for us to understand the foundations of our present churches, for Benedictine prayer was the aim of the rule which is why most of his teaching on the subject comes as a summary of all that has gone before. Prayer is the culmination and the fulfilment of the rule; his communities are called to live prayerfully. De Waal sums this up well:

'Prayer lies at the very heart of the Benedictine life; it holds everything together, it sustains every other activity. It is at the same time root and fruit, foundation and fulfilment. Prayer is the one thing that makes all the rest possible. For praying can never be set apart from the rest of life, it is the life itself. St. Benedict did not ask his monks to take a vow to pray, for he expected prayer to be central in their lives, permeating whatever else they were doing. Prayer is opus dei, the work of God, and nothing whatsoever is to be preferred to it. At least twice St Benedict says nothing must be put before the love of Christ, and he uses precisely the same phrase 'to put nothing before' when he comes to talk of the divine office, as if that is the most excellent witness to the community's love of Christ, the pre-eminent occasion for the expression of that love'.[27]

---

[26] Ibid., 55.
[27] Ibid., 129.

At the beginning of the sixteenth century, the communities of prayer were once again at the heart of Cumbria. By this time, through the gifts of the grateful and desperate, the rich and poor and the nobility and the yeoman classes, the monastic houses have become ever richer. In a little over twenty years, all of this changed forever, and the church lost not only its wealth, but also, and of much greater significance for us, its unity and prayerful heart. For on October 31, 1517, Martin Luther nailed his manifesto of ninety-five articles on the main door of Württemberg Cathedral, and the Western church would never be the same again.

Chapter Four
Our Christian roots

For over a thousand years, there was only one church. Given our present divided and at times quarrelsome churches, it is worth remembering that one simple truth. We used to be one, holy, Catholic and apostolic church. Of course, we quarrelled. We had our differences. The world was violent and cruel; we had to stand up for our beliefs, but being a Christian mattered. How you behaved gave credence to what you believed. Our faith was active. We tried to tell others our 'good news'. Everything was rooted in prayer because our lives were prayerful. Everything we did and said began and ended in prayer. Then we lost it. It is worth pausing to examine exactly what we lost five hundred years ago and why we are still grieving.

Unity

'The coming generations will have less and less patience with the contradiction of Christians split up into different denominations, with all the energy lost defending opposing viewpoints, at a time when the population is rapidly increasing the number of people with no knowledge of God. They will find it intolerable that the best of Christians' time and energy is going to waste justifying their respective positions'.[28]

These words of Brother Roger go to the heart of our common roots. Our church was one church; it was the Body of Christ in this place. Between 451 and 1534, there was only one church in Cumbria. A lot of dates could be chosen for the beginning of the church in our land, but 451 seems to be the best place to begin. The year 451 was when Latinus was remembered at Whithorn

---

[28] *Taize: Brother Roger and His Community* by Rex Brico, Collins, London, 1978 (p. 165).

Growing Spirituality

with the words of faith 'Te Deum Laudemus' on his headstone, a Christian man from a Christian community buried in a Christian grave. Of course, 1534 needs no explanation; the Act of Supremacy passed that year made Henry VIII head of an independent church, beginning what is now called 'The English Reformation'.

Many historians, though, would object. What of the divisions of the seventh century at the Synod of Whitby? What of the Norse invasion which separated Christian communities in the ninth century? What of the Norman imposition of a very different style of church and worship, and the resistance of the ordinary English men and women to it? Yes, of course, there were divisions. We read of divisions in St. Paul's letters to Christians in Corinth, of whom 'one is for Apollos, one for Cephas' and so on. The Tudor historians of Edward VI and Elizabeth's reign were quick to justify their actions by a dishonest claim to authenticity from the past. So the break with Rome could be legitimised by seeing the Synod of Whitby in 664 as a battle between the Celtic Church and the Roman Church. Many authors still make this basic mistake. Yet if the Celtic Church and Roman Church were distinct and separate, where is the evidence? St. Ninian, St. Patrick, St. Wilfrid and St. Cuthbert all went to Rome to pray at St. Peter's tomb; none of them saw any contradiction between the Irish monastic communities and going on pilgrimages to the church in Rome. Benedict Episcop, the mentor of the Venerable Bede, travelled many times to Rome to build up the collection of manuscripts for the communities at Jarrow and Coldingham. There was no contradiction in doing this, for all were one church.

Having said this, of course, there were feuds and disputes, as there have always been in the church. St. Wilfrid was exiled on three occasions for annoying his fellow bishops and various kings. This, though, doesn't represent different denominations but rather that he was a difficult person to be with. The Norse and Danish invasions led to the church being divided because it was physically separated from itself by large tracts of land and population coming under pagan control. What is remarkable is the vibrancy of the church in converting to Christianity each wave of pagan kings and their armies. In Cumbria, we even sent missionaries to the places that were sending warriors to invade this land to convert them to the faith! For the Normans, everything about Anglo-Saxon England was to be ridiculed; again, this was to give credence to their genocide. Only by showing that they came from a superior church could they seek to give any religious value to the violent conquest. There are plenty of reasons for historians to assume that the one thousand years prior to the Reformation were a time of disunity, but the problem is that there is no evidence to back up this claim. Rather, there is evidence to show that the church was united as one community of faith.

Which begs an important question for us: Why are we so content with disunity? This is not our natural state. Our history is as one church, not several churches. Have we become so used to our unnatural state that we have lost sight of where we came from? Brother Roger asked this question nearly fifty years ago:

'Why such discord among Christians? O Church of Christ, are you becoming a secularised locus of spiritual debility, a colourless centre of conformity to worldly fashions, devoid of all signs of meeting with the Risen Christ—salt without savour? Are you becoming a frozen, stereotyped image of the Christian community, a place where people are no longer challenged to take a bold, demanding leap beyond their limitations, an act which would convey to others in the human family their confident expectation of God's coming, and assure them of the

certainty of a presence, the Risen Christ? Are you becoming a place where people are incapable of welcoming others, communicating Christ and living the Gospel in all its freshness? Are you becoming a mere collection of splinter-groups, a place where pluralism turns into fragmentation or simple co-existence? If pluralism runs counter to unanimity, will Christ still find faith upon the earth? [29]

These challenging questions of Brother Roger still have a resonance for us fifty years later. It helps us also to understand that in Cumbria, we are not seeking the ecumenical county out of a desire to create something new; rather, we are longing to return to our natural state in order to demonstrate once more that we are Christ's faithful people.

Living a prayerful life

'Prayer is sitting in the silence until it silences us, choosing gratitude until we are grateful, and praising God until we ourselves are an act of praise'. [30]

Richard Rohr understands prayer to be a way of living, to be about our relationship with God and God's engagement with creation. Too often, prayer is talked of as something we do rather than the realisation that it is something we are: a living relationship with the divine. Thomas Keating expresses this intimacy with God which is vital to every faithful heart:

'We rarely think of the air we breathe, yet it is in us and around us all the time. In similar fashion, the presence of God penetrates us, is all around us, is always embracing us'. [31]

---

[29] Ibid., 168.
[30] Falling Upwards by Richard Rohr, SPCK, London, 2012 (p. 7).

For Rohr and Keating, therefore, the life of faith is a prayerful life. Times of prayer are therefore moments when we stop to recognise the greater truth is at work within us every moment of every day.

For those living in the golden age of the founding saints and their communities in Cumbria, they would have recognised the truth of Rohr's and Keating's words. The Augustinians and Benedictines who built the great prayer houses of the thirteenth, fourteenth and fifteenth centuries knew all about this as well. We have a sure inheritance of the priority of prayer in our Christian lives. As Keating reminds us, it should be as natural to us as breathing in and out. Yet often, our modern church has come to equate all prayer with intercession, as though a recitation of requests is equivalent to a loving relationship. Imagine if this was the sole way in which we spoke to each other every day. Life would be depressing and intolerable after only a few hours. We know that most communication is nonverbal and that rarely we ask anything of each other, rather seeking to share our common story, to tell stories, to laugh and cry. There is nothing wrong with intercessory prayer when seen in its proper role as one small part of a prayerful life.

Those who lived in the Irish communities saw all of life as a prayer. Although the Normans tried to eradicate this intuitive prayerful life, it was never lost. In the nineteenth century, Alexander Carmichael visited the Western Islands of Scotland (which, until the sixteenth century, was one kingdom stretching from Lewis to the Isle of Man). He noticed how the local people prayed as they went about their daily lives.

---

[31] *Centering Prayer* by Thomas Keating, Lantern Books, 2011 (p. 21).

'When the people of the isles came out in the morning to their
tillage, to their fishing, to their farming, or to any of their
various occupations anywhere, they say a short prayer called
"Ceum na Còrach" (The True Way). If the people feel secure
from being overseen or overhead they croon, or sing, or intone
their morning prayer in a pleasing musical manner'.[32]

Carmichael noted down hundreds of prayers covering every
daily activity—lighting the fire, milking the cows, laying the
table and scything grass. For at least six hundred years, this
would have been the practice of Christians in Cumbria as well.
Esther de Waal quotes a typical night prayer:

'May the Light of lights come
To my dark heart from Thy place;
May the Spirit's wisdom come
To my heart's tablet from my Saviour.

Be the peace of the Spirit mine this night,
Be the peace of the Son mine this night,
Be the peace of the Father mine this night,
The peace of all peace be mine this night,
Each morning and evening of my life'.[33]

The patterns of the daily offices used by both Augustinians and
Benedictines are sometimes assumed to be the way of praying
for these communities. This is to misunderstand the practice of
prayer of these great religious houses; rather, these are only the
times of prayer held commonly for both those present physically

---

[32] *The Celtic Vision* by Esther de Waal, DLT, London, 1988 (p.
1).
[33] Ibid., 103.

and those present through eternity. For both Augustinians and
Benedictines who lived and worked in Carlisle, Furness and
Lanercost, all of life was prayer. So there was no separation
between what they were doing in between the daily offices and
the liturgy itself; all of this was the work of prayer. Thomas
Keating comments on this common misunderstanding:

*'The chief thing that separates us from God is the thought that
we are separated from God'.*[34]
If we live in prayer and prayer lives in us, we are always in God
and God in us. This is the great truth that Christians in Cumbria
knew for a thousand years, and it is a truth we need to return to
if our Mission Communities are to be blessed. John V. Taylor
wrote of the vitality of being in a loving relationship with God
in prayer:

*'It has long been my conviction that God is not hugely
concerned as to whether we are religious or not. What matters
to God, and matters supremely, is whether we are alive or not. If
your religion brings you more fully to life, God will be in it; but
if your religion inhibits your capacity for life or makes you run
away from it, you may be sure God is against it, just as Jesus
was'.*[35]

Living a prayerful life is part of our common roots. From the
earliest Christian communities in Crosthwaite, Urswick and St.
Bees, the heartbeat of prayer was known; it was known in the
great houses of Augustinians and Benedictines, as well as in
ordinary faithful hearts. This is a great truth that is handed down
to us. If we are to rediscover our vocation to proclaim the love

---

[34] Keating, op. cit., 22.
[35] *A Matter of Life and Death* by John V. Taylor, SCM, London,
1986 (p. 18).

of God, we need first to feel the heartbeat of love within us and, like Richard Rohr, allow the living of Christ's life in prayer to transform us. Remember Jesus' words to us: *'I have come that you might have life, life in all its fullness'.*[36]

Instinctive Mission
'Mission goes out from God. Mission is God's way of loving and saving the world'.[37]

These words from the 1998 Lambeth Conference remind us that nothing depends upon us. Yet at the very moment, these words were being written when the attendance at Cumbria's churches was continuing to decline; the Decade of Evangelism saw an absolute reduction in church membership. It is tempting to believe that we are living in an age of secularisation, and that there is nothing we can do; it is out of our hands.

Yet if we pause for a moment and consider the world of Latinus in 451, we have so much more that he did and so many more resources with which to assist in God's mission. Our common root is mission; it was, for over a thousand years, the chief outward expression of faith. Prayer was never separated from mission; rather, prayer was always linked with action. What is noticeable about the legacy of St. Ninian, St. Patrick and St. Colmcille was that their missionary zeal was not exceptional; rather, it was ordinary. The story of these founding saints and their desire to express the Gospel in deed is compelling and consistent in all their stories.

'Brendan was abbot of Clonfert, a large monastery in central Ireland. One Lent he went back to the south-western tip of the

---

[36] John 10:10.
[37] Lambeth Conference, 1998 (section II, page 121).

country where he had grown up, and spent the season on top of
a high mountain overlooking the ocean, fasting and praying.
Other pilgrims had set sail before in search of the Island of
Promise and Brendan decided to follow their example. He
recruited fourteen other monks to join him and they built a
coracle out of ox hides tanned with oak bark. We can only infer
their route from the descriptions of the places they visited; and
these suggest they made a giant loop via the Faroe Islands and
Iceland to Newfoundland, returning via the Azores, which they
took to be the Island of Promise'.[38]

The story of St. Brendan shouldn't be understood as simply
being an adventure. Rather, as abbot of a large Irish community,
he demonstrates that instinct to be missional. This is seen over
and over again in the world of the saints and their communities
from the fifth to the eight centuries. St. Columbanus is another
great Irish Christian who, in the sixth century, travelled through
Europe, establishing communities according to Patrick's model.
Columbanus, after journeying through Gaul, Switzerland and
Italy, eventually settled in his dynamic community at Bobbio.
For all these saints, there was nothing strange about taking the
Gospel to places where it had never been spoken before. St.
Cuthbert went to places in Cumbria that no one else dared to go.
Even the most gentle of the saints, Aidan, took the opportunity
every time he met someone new to tell them of Jesus.

Their missionary zeal was instinctive. There is even a story told
in the Anglo-Saxon chronicle of three Irish monks who landed
on the south coast of England in the ninth century and who were
taken to see King Alfred's sheriff. Having fed them and assured
them that Wessex had many Christians, they were sent on their

---

[38] *Celtic Fire* by Robert Van de Weyer, DLT, London, 1993 (p. 23).

Growing Spirituality

way. Two months later, the three monks returned and were taken again to the same sheriff; they apologised for their mistake and went on their way again. Six months later, they were back again; this time, the sheriff's men took them out into the English channel and made sure they truly sailed away, never to return. Nothing better expresses the enthusiasm for mission than a rowing song still sung in Ireland, attributed to St. Columbanus from the sixth century:

'Strong faith and zeal will victory gain,
The old foe breaks his lance in vain,
Think lads, of Christ and echo him.

The King of virtues vowed a prize
For him who wins, for him who tries,
Think lads of Christ and echo him'.[39]

Mission was at the heart of the late medieval world, when the Augustinians and Benedictines were building their abbeys. To take the cross was an act of holiness; successive popes offered absolution from purgatory for those knights prepared to go on crusades. As we have seen, this act of devotion could often result in new religious foundations, the example of St. John le Fleming and Calder Abbey having been described in chapter 3. Of course, to the modern mind, fighting the Crusades is repugnant and rightly so; indeed, often, western Christians fought their eastern brothers and sisters rather than 'liberating the Holy Land'. In reality, whatever the religious motivation for taking up the cross the wars over Palestine was more for the sake of trade and political power. This was as true for Islam as it was for Western Christianity. The destruction of Constantinople in 1204 by knights of the Fourth Crusade, including some from

---

[39] *Columbanus* by Tomás Ó Fiaich, Veritas, Dublin, 1974 (p. 41).

Cumbria, began the slow demise of the Byzantine Empire which, in 1453, was overrun by the Ottomans. As a result, Venice became the supreme power in the Mediterranean and Persia in the east.

For Cumbria, the religious revival prompted by the Fourth Crusade at the beginning of the thirteenth century brought about renewed mission after the social dislocation of the previous one hundred and fifty years. Missionary activity was a sign of holiness; taking the cross inspired many ordinary people to go on pilgrimage. It is no coincidence that the late medieval church saw the increasing popularity of pilgrimage, especially to Glastonbury and Canterbury. For Cumbria, it is believed that St. Bega's cell had a shrine in the fifteenth century with a high cross. Gosforth's high crosses, as well as those at Ireton, Urswick and Bewcastle, were places of pilgrimage, but it is not known whether they were sites of shrines as well.

In looking back to our common roots, it is clear that mission is of central importance. Archbishop Justin had pronounced mission as one of his personal three principles: 'Every church and every Christian has the potential to share their life-transforming faith in Jesus with those around them'. In Cumbria, our rich Christian heritage makes mission one of the three most importance roots of our common Christianity. As the ecumenical county, we always need to remember that for those who went before us from the fifth to the sixteenth century, over a thousand years of witnessing to Christ were founded on three simply truths. Firstly, we are united as one church. Secondly, we live prayerful lives. Thirdly, we are a missionary people, and our mission is as instinctive as breathing in and out.

Growing Spirituality

SECTION B
DISTINCTIVE SPIRITUALITIES

In this second section, the distinctive spiritualities that are evidenced in Cumbria from the four partner churches and the other companion denominations are explored. These three chapters, though, cannot hope to be a survey of all these denominations' distinct ways of believing. Rather, each chapter will pick out significant themes.

Chapter 5 looks at the impact of 1662 and the Great Ejection. The various spiritualities of both the Old Dissent and the Counter-Reformation are very evident in modern Cumbria. The teaching of St. Ignatius of Loyola is of special interest.

Chapter 6 looks at the revival and reform of Methodism, Evangelicalism and the Oxford Movement, tracing their often unseen and surprising influence on the churches in Cumbria.

Chapter 7 attempts to put all of these different and sometimes conflicting spiritualties in a context whereby the positive contribution on the modern church can be recognised.

Lastly, the question is asked of whether these positive qualities added to the common roots identified at the end of Section A can be anything more than the sum total of all that is past.

Chapter Five
Personal journeys

'The impact of reform in the parishes can be brought into sharp focus by looking at a single conservative community, the little Exmoor parish of Morebath, whose priest, Christopher Trychay, was Vicar from 1520 to 1574. His record offers a unique window into a close-knit and largely self-contained community, committed to the old ways but caught up in the revolutionary events. There is certainly no mistaking the Catholic piety of Morebath on the eve of the Reformation'.[40]

Eamon Duffy begins his description of the impact of the Reformation by citing the detailed records of Morebath, Devon. Duffy has done a great service to the history of the church in posing challenging questions to the accepted Tudor history of the Reformation. The seeds sown in Elizabeth I's reign still poison many modern minds. We are still the church of these past hatreds and bigotries. In the Church of England, we might look across the water to Belfast at the Orange Order and the 'marching season' as something foreign to our modern sensibilities, and yet these divisions are to be found in the history of all our denominations.

Duffy, in his challenging conclusion of the final impact of the Reformation upon Morebath, gives us a clue as to why the Christian church changed so greatly after 1563 in England. The Elizabethan Protestant accommodation, though often seen as the compromise that laid the foundation of the Church of England, came at a great cost.

---

[40] *The Stripping of the Altars* by Eamon Duffy, Yale, London, 1992 (pp. 497–8).

'The price for such accommodation was the death of the past it sought to conserve. If Protestantism was transformed, so was traditional religion. The imaginative world was gradually obliterated from wall and window. Cranmer's somberly magnificent prose, read week by week, entered and possessed their minds and became the fabric of their prayer. And more strident words entered their minds and hearts too, the polemic of Foxe's Acts and Monuments, and of a thousand no-popery sermons, a relentless torrent carrying away the landmarks of a thousand years. By the end of the 1570s a generation was growing up which had known nothing else, which believed the Pope to be Antichrist, the Mass a mummery which did not look back to the Catholic past as their own, but another country, another world'.[41]

Duffy, in presenting perhaps a more accurate picture of the English Reformation, helps us to understand the English Civil War and the Commonwealth in its proper context. The years 1642 to 1660 represent the culmination of all the unresolved hatreds of both sides of the Tudor years. The ultimate failure of both Thomas and Oliver Cromwell, in different ways, is represented by the restoration of Charles II to the throne and 'The Great Ejection' of 1662.

Henry VIII had greedily exploited Martin Luther's principled protest against the expansionist papacy to fill the Crown's treasury with the wealth of the monasteries. The radical Calvinism of his son wrecked the church and, together with the extreme reaction of Mary, left England shattered and bewildered. It was this fragmented nation that Elizabeth's accommodation sought to address. Her settlement, ruthlessly applied with a network of spies and informers, kept the church

---

[41] Ibid., 593.

together and the nation obediently submissive. In the reigns of James I and Charles I, there was no such control, and the Stuarts' flirtation with the Counter-Reformation of St. Charles Borromeo gave a political cause for the Puritans, Congregationalists and Anabaptists to rally around. Whether or not Oliver Cromwell shared the religious sympathies of many of his followers, there can be no doubt of the intense passion of his own personal conviction. It was said that 'no man in battle, not even his own troops, could look him in the eye for fear that he would strike them down'[42]. Here was a religious zealot as the supreme ruler of England like none before, yet for all his pride and passion, the English revolution came to nothing. Even as he was buried with all the trappings of a divinely appointed monarch, his generals were petitioning the hated son of the king he had executed to return and become king again.

The period from 1534 to 1660, in many ways, is the most confusing of our history. By 1660, though, the nation had enough of war and of religion. The choice for every citizen was clear: conform or be expelled. What this meant was to be exiled within the nation; when the legislation was approved by parliament in 1662, the impact was severe and uncompromising. Only those who accepted the Elizabethan settlement could now work for the government, be a member of parliament, be clergy, magistrate or court official, read for a degree and live anywhere. Those who would not accept bishops, be communicate members of the Church of England, only use the Prayer Book, read the Authorised Version of the Bible and acknowledge the monarch as the head of the church were expelled—not simply from their churches and occupations, but also from their homes. So began a period of a hundred and seventy five years where dissenters and

---

[42] God's Englishman by Christopher Hill, Penguin, 1980 (p. 152).

Roman Catholics met in secret for fear of betrayal to worship and had to seek occupations in trade and industry to survive. The 1662 Act, for example, forbade any dissenter or Roman Catholic from living within ten miles of Carfax Tower in Oxford. As a result, Oxford today is surrounded by towns long associated with manufacturing industries Banbury, Bicester, Thame, Abingdon and Witney; each have their own non-conformist and Roman Catholic histories. The impact on the Church of England was dire. Stifled by the restrictions of the 1662 Act, with its energy sapped by over a century of violence and hatred, it began its long decline into the torpor of the Hanoverian church.

And yet from the very unpromising succession of reforming disasters came some of the jewels of the present church. This has often been the outcome in the history of the church, both in Cumbria and farther afield. Latinus, in 451, died praising God in a land full of dangers, but within two hundred years, the whole country was Christian. The vibrant Anglo-Saxon culture and church was brutally destroyed by the Conqueror, and yet within one hundred and fifty years, abbeys were being built, and contemplative prayer was at the heart of the faithful life. In the same way, after 1662, there began the seeds of religious revival among the dissenters and in the Roman Catholic Church, patterns of believing and spirituality which speak to the modern world and form the basis of the contemporary denominations.

The Society of Friends

'Be patterns, be examples in all countries, places, islands, nations wherever you come; that your carriage and life may preach among all sorts of people, and to them; then you will come to walk cheerfully over the world, answering that of God

in everyone; whereby in them you may be a blessing, and make the witness of God in them to bless you'.[43]

These words of George Fox, probably preached in 1656, express powerfully the core belief of the Society of Friends, commonly known as 'The Quakers'. George Fox and the story of Quakerism is rooted in Cumbria. George Fox, though, did not come from Cumbria; rather, he was born in Fenny Drayton, Leicestershire. At the age of twenty-six, he came to a strong personal experience of an inner light. In these years, of course, England was in turmoil as the king fought Parliament. The battles of the English Civil War were the bloodiest ever witnessed on English soil. The brutality and savagery of the killing was typical of civil wars throughout history. In 1642, Carlisle declared itself for the crown, but after a terrible siege lasting eight months, it finally surrendered to a parliamentary army under the notorious General Lesley, many of its citizens dying from starvation or as a result of the revenge inflicted by Lesley's troops on its surrender. Six years later, the city again declared for the king, but this time, there was no siege but, rather, a frontal assault which left Carlisle in ruins and most of its people either exiled or dead. This was George Fox's world and explains the absolute focus of Quakerism on pacifism. At the end of his life he recalled writing to Cromwell to express his outrage:

'I was moved of the Lord to write a paper to the Protector, Oliver Cromwell; wherein I did, in the presence of the Lord God, declare that I denied the wearing or drawing of a carnal sword or any other outward weapon, against him or any man; and that I was sent of God to stand a witness against all

---

[43] *The Works of George Fox, Volume Three* by George Fox, Forgotten Books, London, 2015 (p. 5).

violence, and against the works of darkness; and to turn people from darkness to light; and to bring them from the causes of war and fighting, to the peaceable gospel. When I had written what the Lord had given me to write, I set my name to it, and gave it to Captain Drury to hand to Oliver Cromwell which he did'.[44]

George Fox had a profound religious experience in 1652; seeking peace and solitude, he climbed Pendle Hill and here, had a profound experience of God's presence. As a result, he began to preach in public places and began to draw to himself many of those who were disillusioned with the violent religious division in the English Commonwealth under the Lord Protector Oliver Cromwell. George's experience in 1652 led him to the unmistakable conclusion that each person should seek a direct, unmediated communion with the Divine, for he stated, 'Christ is come to teach his people himself'[45]. This is a belief still clearly stated in the modern 'Quaker faith and practice':

'Just as Quakers do not limit the service of God to certain times, or places, or people, so they do not have a set-apart priesthood. There is no need for any specific person to be designated prophet, priest or church leader'.[46]

Despite the peaceful nature of Quakerism, its members suffered greatly in 1662. George Fox and his followers were seen as dangerous radicals set at destablising the newly restored monarchy. As a result, they were subjected to a systematic persecution depriving many not only of their jobs but also of their liberty. George Fox himself was often thrown into prison, including on two occasions by the Baronet Sir Daniel Fleming

---

[44] Ibid., 247.
[45] Ibid., 122.
[46] *Quaker Faith and Practice*, Quaker Books, 1999 (27.36).

who lived at Rydal Hall. Cumbria, though, is vitally important for the worldwide family of Quakerism, as this county is often described as its 'birthplace'. In 1655, George Fox met Margaret Fell. Margaret made her home at Swarthmoor Hall (near Ulverston in the south of Cumbria), a centre for the Society of Friends. Here, she supported George in travelling nationwide, gathering contributions to create 'The Kendal Fund'. George and Margaret eventually married, and by the time of his death in 1691, the fund was supporting sixty preachers. Margaret Fell is often called, with good reason, the 'Mother of Quakerism'.

Quakerism remains a small but important part of the whole church. It is, though, often difficult for members of other churches to understand. This is due to the lack of any doctrinal statement specific to Quakerism. The unique nature of Quakerism is explained simply by the Quaker Information Centre:

'Worldwide, the vast majority of Friends confess an orthodox Christian faith. Friends' emphasis has always been on the role of the immediate guidance of the Holy Spirit, however, most Friends believe that the Spirit is unchanging and will not contradict itself. On this basis, the Christian Scriptures and tradition are highly esteemed as testimony to God's relationship with our spiritual ancestors. Crucially, because most Friends consider the Scriptures to be inspired by God, the Bible is helping in weighing whether new inward guidance comes from the Spirit of God or from another source. Friends aim at an inward knowledge of the Spirit—both individually and in our Meetings. The core of our faith is our living relationship with

and the obedience to God, not merely the rote recitation of creeds or performance of rituals'.[47]

Quakerism shouldn't be regarded as distinct from the Christian church. Indeed, many Christians combine attendance at a Friends meeting with being a member of a particular denomination. There is nothing strange in doing this, as Quakerism was never meant to become an alternative to the church. Rather, it is a way of believing and living which marks out its distinctive spirituality. For Friends, 'it is how we live and how we treat one another that truly expresses what we believe; 'The deeper realities of our faith are beyond precise verbal formulation, and our way of worship based on silent waiting testifies to this'.[48]

The United Reformed Church
Of all the partners in the present ecumenical county of Cumbria, the United Reformed Church (URC) is the most recent to be formed, but its heritage is older than the Quakers. The URC was created in 1972 from a union of the Presbyterian Church of England and the majority of English Congregational churches. Later on, in 1981, the URC was joined by the Reformed Association of the Churches of Christ and finally, in 2000, by the Congregational Union of Scotland. As a result of these unions, the URC is rooted in Presbyterianism. In England, this was quite distinct from the Scottish Presbyterian movement, although in Cumbria at present, both strands are represented in

---

[47] 'What do Quakers believe?' by Q. Cadmin, Earlham School of Religion, Quaker Information Centre, 2011, www.quakerinfo.org.

[48] 'Advices and Queries', The Yearly Meeting of the Religious Society of Friends in Britain, 1995 (pp. 3–4).

the ecumenical county through the URC and Church of Scotland.

English Presbyterianism first emerged in 1558 and was rooted in the return of exiles to the country following Elizabeth I's accession in that year. These exiles began to campaign for church reform along the lines of the churches they had seen in Europe which sought a pattern of church life rooted in scripture and a church without bishops but rather the local community, being organised by presbyters drawn from the congregation. However, Presbyterianism ran counter to the Elizabethan settlement, and many of those exiled soon returned to Europe. Those Presbyterians who did remain faced imprisonment and execution. Many saw themselves as the natural allies of puritan groups; however, this was set to change. In 1640, twelve bishops were imprisoned, and the *Grand Remonstrance* was published. On December 11, the Rood and Branch Petition was presented to Parliament in a march of fifteen thousand people. As a result of the march and petition, the Westminster Assembly of Divines was established, and in turn, their debates culminated in the 1645 Act which required every parish to have a 'congregational assembly' of ruling elected elders. Up until this point, English Presbyterianism seemed to have got everything it had been campaigning for since 1558.

In 1649, the alliance between Presbyterianism and puritanism dramatically broke apart over the trial and execution of King Charles I. Despite having achieved a great deal of the reform they had been seeking, the Presbyterians remained loyal to the monarchy. It is ironic, therefore, that they suffered so badly under the Restoration in 1660. The 1662 Act of Uniformity proved to be unacceptable, mainly due to the restoration of bishops. On St. Bartholomew's Day, over two thousand ministers were evicted from their parishes which. in most cases, meant that they became homeless as well. The day became known as 'The Great Ejection', and from that day on, Presbyterians became persecuted. Unable to worship in churches, they began to use homes or out-buildings, calling their places of worship 'chapels'. In many cases, they continued illegally to baptise, marry and bury members of the chapels and to preach to large gatherings. Presbyterians came to be hated by the reformed Church of England, partly because of the large number of ministers who had been expelled and who had been former clergy. There was a hatred of the repopulated bishoprics. Of course, Presbyterians represented a substantial threat, as their chapels often appeared to be alternate parish churches.

The Presbyterian congregations of the seventeenth and eighteenth centuries were often more creative than the stifled Church of England. Philip Henry was one of those ejected on St. Bartholomew's Day in 1662. As he was a moderately wealthy man, he was able to provide for his family and send his son Matthew to school. It was his son Matthew who became a leading light of Presbyterianism. Although wanting to go into law, he was prevented from doing so by his Presbyterian allegiance and so trained as a minister; his influence first as a preacher in the northwest was immense before he went on in 1687 to be minister of a congregation at Chester. Between 1708 and 1710, he wrote his six volume, *Exposition of the Old and New Testaments*. John Wesley wrote of Matthew Henry some fifty years later, remarking on his influence:

'He is allowed by all competent judges to have become a person of strong understanding, of various learning, of solid piety, and much experience in the ways of God. His exposition is generally clear and intelligible, the thoughts being expressed in plain words. It does not entertain us with vain speculations, but is

practical throughout: and usually spiritual too teaching us how to worship God, not in form only, but in spirit and in truth'.[49]

Henry is an example of the vitality of much Presbyterian teaching and church life in stark contrast to the dire state of the Church of England following the 1688 Glorious Revolution which saw the national church become part of the political structure of the nation. William Wordsworth, a century afterwards, complained regularly of preachers who were more interested in 'the affairs of the King's court' than in the affairs of God.

The URC has inherited, of course, from its Presbyterian roots a strong sense of its congregational identity and seeking a common identity as Christ's body in each place. For George Fox, it was the 'inner light' and the active discernment of Christ in one another that was the clear theological focus. For the URC, the sense in which the church is only the church if everyone plays their part is grounded in the understanding of the early church and their own rootedness in scripture. The URC website states: 'The Church sets a high value on individual conscience and the ability of its members reaching a common understanding'. The minister and church elders are seen as equals and the leadership is provided by one who is 'first among equals'. In many ways, the URC is more conservative than other denominations in its doctrine, its theological statement being quite clear: 'The United Reformed Church shares the Trinitarian tradition and creeds of all major denominations and the Bible is taken to be the supreme authority for the Church'.

---

[49] *Preface to Matthew Henry's Old Testament Notes* by John Wesley, 1765.

Growing Spirituality

It is the supreme authority of the Bible that is also strongly represented in the Reformed Churches of Christ which joined the URC in 1981. The original Churches of Christ, founded by Scottish Presbyterian Alexander Campbell, were an attempt to restore the teaching of the church to a sound biblical base. Although his influence was largely to be felt in Western Virginia, the Churches of Christ came to have a strong influence upon the churches that eventually joined with the URC. More locally congregational than the Presbyterian churches, the Churches of Christ were more like 'free churches', non-denominational and non-institutional. The Churches of Christ held to 'the priesthood of all believers', rejecting any titles for any role played by any members of the church. In some ways, the Churches of Christ were closer to the Baptists, insisting on a believer's baptism and regarding discipleship as the observance to the proclaimed facts of the Gospel. For the Churches of Christ, the process of salvation follows six steps, each one rooted in scripture: to be properly taught, to believe, to repent, to confess that Jesus is God's Son, to be baptised and to live faithfully.

All of these elements go to make up the URC and, as such, bring a distinctive voice into the ecumenical county. The URC says of the modern church:

'Who is the United Reformed Church? We are a family of Christians, worshipping in the name of Jesus in about 1500 local churches from Orkney to Cornwall. "Reformed" means that we delight in the Bible, we do not fear change, and we try to run our churches in ways that take everyone's insight and contribution seriously. "United" is an important part of our story. We started when English Presbyterians merged with English and Welsh Congregationalists in 1972. Churches of Christ joined in 1981 and Scottish Congregationalists in 2000.

We still work as closely as we can with Christians of all traditions and styles. And we are one "Church". We aim to grow through supporting one another and taking decisions together'.[50]

Ignatian Spirituality

Before the Reformation, there were no Roman Catholics. The term 'Roman Catholic' is only used post-1517; before this time, we were all simply 'Catholics'. This chapter is about the legacy of the separate spiritualties, not just of the Reformation, but also of the Counter-Reformation. St. Charles Borromeo, as Archbishop of Milan, worked with St. Ignatius of Loyola, amongst others, to resist the efforts of Protestant Reformers. Borromeo was responsible for the large-scale founding of seminaries for the education of priests in the belief that education would counter the influence of the reformers. He also established the lay order of St. Ambrose in order to encourage greater engagement among the laity. However, it was his support of Ignatius, his advocacy of the 'Spiritual Exercises' and the promotion of the Jesuit Order that is of most significant for Cumbria.

Following 1662, there was very little activity by Roman Catholics in Cumbria. The first recorded unofficial Mass is mentioned in 1781, but it wasn't until the Catholic Emancipation Act of 1829 that churches could be built in the county. From this date, the Roman Catholic Church has played an active and prominent part in the life of the county. From the beginning of the ecumenical county, the Roman Catholic Bishop of Lancaster has played a leading role in building strong ecumenical relationships. Presently, there are several 'church-sharing schemes' in operation, and Bishop Michael is one of the

---

[50] www.urc.org.uk

Growing Spirituality

signatories to the Letters of Companionship signed in 2011 and in 2016. The support given by the Roman Catholic Diocese of Lancaster could hardly be greater, given the wider issues of division between the denominations nationally and internationally.

For contemporary Cumbria, the importance of Ignatian Spirituality should not be overlooked. The Spiritual Exercises are used by many Christians, most of whom are not Roman Catholics. The prayer of Examen is used by those training to be Spiritual Directors, and many people use the practice of Gospel Contemplation without realising its origin. So if we are to positively include all the spiritual fruits of our separate denominations, it is necessary to consider St. Ignatius. He was born in 1491 in Spain, one of thirteen children, and as with many of the sons of the aristocracy, he became a knight. Seriously injured in 1521, he had a series of spiritual awakenings over the months of his convalescence. His attention focused on the life of Jesus and of all saints, who cheered him during his painful recovery. St. Ignatius believed in the importance of education and disciplined study to effect change. Having made a pilgrimage to Jerusalem, he returned home and studied for two years in Barcelona. Even by this time, he had attracted followers, and so the Spiritual Exercises were written for this embryonic fellowship.

The Spiritual Exercises were conceived by Ignatius to be threefold. There is the relationship between the Spiritual Director and Exercitant (the person who follows the exercises), the Exercitant and God, and God and the Spiritual Director. In this way, the prayer is always guided and the practice of prayer is never solitary in the Spiritual Exercises. The full set of exercises takes place over thirty days, and therefore, these are rarely completed more than once or twice in a lifetime. The impact of this guided prayer can be transformative, yet the various elements of the Exercises can be used by anyone in their daily lives. Of these, the prayer of Examen is most widely used. Jim Manney's book on the prayer is a very accessible way into this spiritual practice, and he describes it as follows:

'The examen is a method of reviewing your prayer in the presence of God. Here it is in a nutshell:
1. *Ask God for light. I want to look at my day with God's eyes, not merely my own.*
2. *Give thanks. Be grateful.*
3. *Review the day. I carefully look back on the day just completed being guided by the Holy Spirit.*
4. *Face your shortcomings. I face up to what is wrong, in my life and me.*
5. *Look toward the day to come. I ask where I need God in the day to come* '[51]

The ways of praying, first used by St. Ignatius and his followers, resonate in the modern mind. His almost-conversational style is so helpful to those put off by the formality of Christian worship. The concentration on the person of Jesus is refreshing and simple amid all the 'doctrines' of the church. Our present Pope Francis is, of course, a Jesuit and follows the spiritual practices of St. Ignatius; he demonstrates this 'down-to-earth' rooted spirituality. Jim Manney sums it up:

'The examen isn't the only way to pray but it's a way that everyone can pray. It banishes the abstract and relishes the concrete. It is inexhaustible. It treats every moment of everyday

---

[51] *A Simple Life-changing Prayer* by Jim Manney, Loyola Press, Chicago, 2011 (p. 1).

Growing Spirituality

as a blessed time when God can appear. It's a way to find God in all things'.[52]

Personal Journeys

Whilst the impact of the Reformation may have been to fragment and divide the church, one of the positive outcomes was the development of new forms of spirituality which continue to support individuals' and communities' journeys in faith. Quakerism, Presbyterianism and Ignatian Spirituality have this in common. The recognition of the 'inner light', the seeking in all things and the daily encounter with God through the Examen all assist in the personal journeys of the faithful.

---

[52] Ibid., 4.

Chapter Six
Revival and growth

On May 24, 1738, John Wesley attended a service in Aldgate, London. In this service, he had an experience of his faith being reawakened. 'I felt my heart strangely warmed', he wrote of his experience. 'I felt I did trust in Christ, in Christ alone, for salvation'.[53] His brother Charles wrote of the same experience, but more poetically, in the words of the hymn 'And can it be':
'My chains fell off, my heart was free,
I rose, went forth, and followed thee'[54]

The following year, John and Charles joined with George Whitefield, who, like them, had been trained as a Church of England minister and had been part of 'The Holy Club' at Oxford University in 1732. George had begun preaching in the open air to anyone who would gather to hear him speak. He encouraged John and Charles to join him. Eventually, they went with George and realised the potential of this ministry. For John, this was to become his lifelong ministry. He wrote in his journal: 'I look upon the whole world as my parish'.

The success of George Whitfield and the Wesley brothers drew other young preachers, and so John set up three preaching houses in Bristol, London and Newcastle. Equally significant societies were formed in each place where their preaching was gladly received. John Wesley visited Cumbria on twenty-six occasions, partially due to travelling from Whitehaven to the Isle of Man and Ireland. However, he was invited to Whitehaven

---

[53] 'What is Methodism', Cumbria Wesley Historical Society, Carlisle, 2010 (p. 4).
[54] *Hymns and Psalms*, Methodist Publishing House, London, 1983 (lines from Hymn 216, 'And can it be').

Growing Spirituality

originally by Joseph Cownley, and it was the first society founded in the county in 1749.

George Whitfield went to America in 1740, and when Charles married in 1749, he gave up travelling, and settled into a parish in Bristol. This left John Wesley to inspire a whole generation of preachers. By the time of his death in 1791, it is estimated that seventy-two thousand were members of local societies and circuits around the country. So what was it in Wesley's preaching that attracted so many? Wesleyan spirituality is about holiness. He speaks of grace in four ways: prevenient, converting, sanctifying and glorifying. In this way, he shows his rootedness in the teaching of the Church Fathers. Wesley demonstrates a great love for Patristics. Steve Harper summarises Wesley's spirituality:

'Through prevenient grace, we awaken to God. Through converting grace, we attach to God. Through sanctifying grace we advance in God. And finally, in glorifying grace, we make the transition from earth to heaven, where we arrive in heaven to forever glorify God'.[55]

Wesley's preaching was therefore about transformation. He spoke of the need for the inner life to change our lifestyle and behaviour. The local societies were much more than a simple meeting place for ordinary working people; they were a place to share experiences of God and the difficulty in walking the way of holiness. The path to holiness was through perfect love, so his message was as much about how to be a Christian as what a believer should believe.

---

[55] *The Way to Heaven: The Gospel According to John Wesley* by Steve Harper, Zondervan, 2003 (p. 22).

In helping those who joined the earliest societies, Wesley offered the idea of a quadrilateral. Jeff Thomas explains this most clearly:

'Wesley believed that the living core of the Christian faith was revealed in scripture, illumined by tradition, vivified in personal experience and confirmed by reason. Scripture, however, is primary, revealing the Word of God so far as it is necessary for our salvation'.[56]

The class meetings which were fundamental to the life of his societies, are key to this practical reflection on life, and he often said of the members that they were to 'watch over one another in love'. As a result of Wesley's desire to live a holy life guided by perfect love, it is perhaps not surprising that a key aspect of his societies was their care for those most in need. Wesley said 'the Gospel of Christ knows no religion but social care'. One of his great concerns was health; in 1747, he published *Primitive Physick* which gave practical advice of how to avoid illness. By his death, there had been twenty-three editions. He supported William Wilberforce in seeking the abolition of the slave trade. He encouraged reading societies for adults and Sunday schools for children, as well as seeing the importance of Christians addressing the social evils of the day in local politics.

In reading the first three pages of this chapter, it can be assumed that I am writing about the foundation of the Methodist Church, and yet that assumption would be wrong, for everything described so far falls within the Church of England. Wesley died in 1791, forty years before there was complete religious freedom in Britain. Perhaps because his grandfather was a dissenter,

---

[56] Wesleyan Spirituality by Jeff Thomas (an extract from a talk given to the 'Nourishing the Soul' course on June 18, 2016).

Wesley was keen at all times to call himself 'a Church of England man'. Wesley kept a close eye on the movement which was ridiculed and mocked as 'methodism'. His preachers met each year in conference and would discuss all areas of the work of this movement, but he never saw it as a substitute for the church. Indeed, members of his movement were forbidden from meeting at times when church services were being held. The Methodist denomination came after his death. Probably the best tribute to him is in his own words:

'Do all the good you can. By all the means you can. In all the ways you can. In all the places you can. At all the times you can. To all the people you can. As long as ever you can'.[57]

As much as he was a charismatic leader, John Wesley left an impossible void to fill. Whilst Wesley could command the loyalty and respect of his followers, 'methodism' remained a renewal movement. From the time of his death, the movement almost immediately began to fragment. These, though, were uncertain and difficult times; the 1790s were years of repression by a government worried about the revolutionary ideas from France. This popular movement looked to George III's government, a dangerous stepping stone to political revolution. The first to break away from the movement were Alexander Kilham and William Thom, who formed the Methodist New Connexion in 1797. Soon after this first breakaway, in 1811, Hugh Bourne and William Clowes formed the Primitive Methodists, and this further split in 1815 with the Bible Christians being created (who, in turn, had links with the Churches of Christ). Over the next fifty years, there was an almost bewildering number of divisions and mergers until 1857, when three denominations remained: Wesleyan Methodists,

---

[57] Harper, op., cit., 152.

United Methodists and Primitive Methodists. The Methodist Church that forms one of the partners of the ecumenical county wasn't formed until 1932 with the amalgamation of these three parts. Cumbria, like many parts of the north of England, can still trace these splits in Methodism pointing to the variety of chapels, often two or three buildings in the same village. Yet it cannot be denied that Methodism, in all its forms, was imbued with the same passion for mission and growth that Wesley demonstrated, even if it couldn't live up to his calling of living in perfect love, at least in terms of fellow Methodists.

Revival

It is strange to include one of the companion denominations so late in the story of the churches in Cumbria. Yet in many ways, Baptists struggled to make any impression in Cumbria due to the strength of Quakers and the revival of the church through Wesley's Methodism. There are references, though, to Baptist congregations in the seventeenth century, although numbering just a few families. In 1747, Archdeacon Waugh could only find six families, and forty years later, there were only twenty-eight 'baptists' compared to nearly two hundred 'presbyterians' and over four hundred 'quakers'. These very small churches were based at Carlisle, Cockermouth, Lowick, Great Broughton and Hawkshead. However, there are examples of old foundations. The chapel at Hawkshead Hill was founded in 1678, when a small group, including John Dickinson, John Rawlinson and Thomas Braithwite, pledged themselves, 'first giving ourselves to the Lord and to one another according to the will of God, promising by the help of divine Grace to walk as becometh saints in the order of the Gospel'. In 1709, under the Act of Toleration, the building was registered as 'a meeting place'. William Wordsworth was at school in Hawkshead and noted, 'In the first cluster of houses we come to, named Hawkshead Hill, stands a meeting-house by the road side belonging to a congregation of Anabaptists'. However, on several occasions, the chapel ceased to be a place of worship and, in its present form, was reopened in 1977.

Though the numbers of Baptists were only small, their growth throughout was consistent with a revival in the church. By 1902, the numbers attending the five chapels of West Cumberland had grown to 396. It is often assumed that church attendance in the past was much higher than it is today. The Religious Census shows that in West Cumberland, the Church of England had only 9,475 attendees, and the next highest denomination (Wesleyan, Primitive and United) were the Methodists with 7,664. By this time, the number of Quakers had dwindled to 107[58]. Having said this, the revival sweeping the Church of England also had its impact upon Cumbria.

The evidence of the slave trade is to be found throughout Cumbria. The large houses of the slave owners, built by the wealth created by the eighteenth century triangular trade, are well known. What is less frequently mentioned is the part played by individuals in Cumbria as part of the campaign to end this trade. Both William Wilberforce and Thomas Clarkson came regularly to Cumbria, and both were friends of the Wordsworths. Linked with the extensive Quaker influence in Cumbria, these two leading campaigners in the late eighteenth century brought the argument right to the front doors of the slave traders. The record office in Kendal has several examples of posters put up by the abolitionists for rallies through the town. Henry Brougham from Penrith, as Member of Parliament, joined with Wilberforce to campaign for abolition. Even after the success of the campaign, Cumbria continued to campaign for the freedom of all slaves. James Cropper, a wealthy Quaker

---

[58] *West Cumberland Times*, December 1, 1902.

manufacturer in the 1820s, paid for a national campaign led by Thomas Clarkson to end slavery throughout the empire. He even bought thousands of bottles and filled them with sugar that came from areas of the world where slavery had been abolished, perhaps the first example of fairly traded goods. The Clapham Sect, of which Wilberforce was a leading member and which inspired a revival in the church's empathy and compassion for the poor, touched Cumbria.

Of course, the revival in the church was to be found not only in the Wesleyan preachers and the social justice campaigns of the Clapham Sect. The revival of the church also came in broadening appeal, personal piety and devotion. Inspired through poetry and hymn writing, Cumbria also played a role in this revival. Wordsworth, although famously dismissive of clergy who gossip about London society instead of preaching the Gospel, found in the landscape glimpses of the divine. In 1798, he wrote these words on being moved by the landscape above Tintern Abbey:

'That on the banks of this delightful stream
We stood together; and that I, so long
A worshipper of Nature, hither came,
Unwearied in that service: rather say
With warmer love, oh! with far deeper zeal
Of holier love. Nor wilt thou then forget,
That after many wanderings, many years
Of absence, these steep woods and lofty cliffs,
And this green pastoral landscape, were to me
More dear, both for themselves and for thy sake'.[59]

---

[59] *The Major Works* of William Wordsworth, OUP, Oxford, 1984 (p. 160).

Growing Spirituality

The romantic poetry that came to be associated with Cumbria spoke to Christians whose own revival was founded partly in the poetry of Charles Wesley's hymns and in other contemporary writers. Dora, Wordsworth's beloved daughter, in her friendship with Charlotte Elliott in 1835, inspired one of the most famous hymns associated with Cumbria:

'Just as I am - without one plea,
But that Thy blood was shed for me,
And that Thou bidst me come to Thee,
-O Lamb of God, I come!

'Just as I am - of that free love
The breadth, length, depth, and height to prove,
Here for a season, then above,
-O Lamb of God, I come![60]

This hymn is even alluded to in the headstone of Dora which pictures the Lamb of God.

Anglo-Catholicism
Increasingly throughout the nineteenth century, the growth of the Oxford Movement had a significant impact upon Cumbria. Built in 1854, St. Mary's Ambleside was designed by Sir Gilbert Scott. The church contained carvings of fourteen 'local saints'; Ambleside was one of several churches influenced by the pre-Raphaelite artist Edmund Burne-Jones. Nine churches in Cumbria featured stained glass windows by Burne-Jones, among them Irton and Lanercost, Troutbeck being the most famous. He left his mark in many other churches through the work of his

---

[60] *The English Hymnal*, OUP, London, 1933 number 316, page 439).

apprentice Henry Holiday, who was commissioned for many stained glass windows not only in Ambleside but in places seemingly far removed from the Oxford Movement, such as St. Oswald's Grasmere. However the renewed interest not only in architecture and decoration brought by the Oxford Movement was only part of the revival in the church's liturgy. The stultification of worship in 1662 was replaced by an increasing interest in ritual, music, colour and the festivals of the church's year. The Tractarian movement increasingly influenced Church of England churches in Cumbria throughout the nineteenth century, encouraging the use of altar clothes, robed choirs, vestments and the more frequent celebration.

Following Catholic Emancipation in 1829, Roman Catholics began to build churches throughout the county, one of the earliest being St. Cuthbert's at Wigton in 1837, built in the Tractarian style of gothic revival. Soon after, Pugin, in 1840, designed Our Lady and St. Wilfrid's Church at Warwick Bridge, and his son built churches at Whitehaven and Cleator Moor. Gothic revival churches followed in Cockermouth, St. Bees, Great Langdale and Kendal. The growth of the church throughout the county was linked to church-building resulting from religious freedom, increasing wealth and a desire by many church congregations to make a statement about the authenticity of their belief. One question that remains from this time is whether all these church buildings which were constructed during the Victorian revival, were ever filled.

In 1851, Thomas Mann conducted a survey of church attendance which scandalised Victorian society. He found that only 17 percent of the population attended church at Whitsun in England. The conclusion reached by the church and national leaders was that there were not enough places available, and so began the great building boom of the 1850s through the 1880s which saw many new churches built in towns and cities. Not all church leaders, though, agreed with this remedy, Professor F. D. Maurice of Kings College London advised the government 'to dig rather than to build'[61]. In other words, he believed that it was the spiritual health of the church that would bring growth, rather than simply adding more buildings. Many churchman came to share Professor Maurice's view, and it is a tragic fact that few of these Victorian churches have ever served a vibrant congregation. In South Yorkshire at Wentworth, a vast Victorian church was put up to seat a thousand people, but at that time, there were only four hundred residents, and now that the community has dwindled, so that everyone who lives there can easily sit in the chancel. The Evangelical Revival and Anglo-Catholic settlement movements of the late Victorian church brought a new energy into the church. The practical missionary work of church leaders such as William Walsham, who took steps to bring the church to ordinary working people, was legendary. He even held services on the factory floor and at the bottom of shafts in coal mines, so that the church was to be found in the daily lives of everyone.

The Salvation Army
There are few Victorians who had such a passion for the good news of Jesus to be brought into the darkest places of society than William Booth. He was born in 1829 in Nottingham, and the example of his father haunted him. Booth later said of him, 'My father was born into poverty, he determined to grown rich, and he did. He grew very rich, because he lived without God and simply worked for money; and when he lost it all, his heart broke with it, and he died miserably'.[62] At the age of thirteen, he

---

[61] *The Kingdom of Christ* by F. D. Maurice, 1852 (p. 21).
[62] *William Booth: Soup, Soap and Salvation* by Janet and Geoff Benge, YWAM Publishing, 2002 (p. 11).

worked in pawnbrokers in the most destitute part of the city, where life expectancy for women was barely thirty and for men, only ten years more. The experience gave him a passion for the poorest in society. Joining the Methodist New Connexion, Booth became a preacher, meeting his wife Catherine on his travels. Together, they formed the Christian Mission in the darkest part of east London: Whitechapel. William and Catherine understood their mission to be on behalf of the whole church but there was considerable opposition to their work from local churches. Their converts were shunned and were not welcomed by the mainstream denominations. In 1878, Booth said of his growing mission:

'We are a salvation people—this is our specialty—getting saved and keeping saved, and then getting somebody else saved'.[63]

Ridiculed as 'the salvation army', Booth adopted the name for this mission and sought to spread its influence across the country. Travelling the whole length of Britain, he came to Cumbria and encouraged the establishment of the mission in Carlisle and in places were poverty was greatest. Booth travelled overseas as far as New Zealand. At the time of his death, the Salvation Army had nearly sixteen thousand full-time officers and was present amongst the poorest in fifty-eight countries.

Independent Churches

Into the twentieth century, Cumbria had witnessed the growth of many independent churches. These tend to be strongly biblically based and relating to one locality. Some are part of wider fellowships, such as 'The King's Church'. Others are purely a locally based Christian fellowship. It is difficult to generalise as to one reason why individuals have felt the need to form these

---

[63] Ibid., 123.

churches. Often, it is simply because the traditional churches are not accessible to new ways of worship; sometimes, there is a desire to have much more conservative moral teaching based on scripture, and occasionally, it is a breakdown in local relationships. One of the most reassuring aspects of the ecumenical county is the strong desire on all sides for all Christians to be included. So although the 2016 Declaration of an Ecumenical covenant involved four signatories to the covenant itself, and four more to a letter of companionship, the other independent churches are working together locally in projects such as HOPE Carlisle, and representatives do attend the annual church leaders' gatherings.

Revival and Growth

The renewed spirituality which swept up Cumbria in the late eighteenth century and which brought about the growth of churches in the nineteenth century, has given rise to a variety of distinctive denominations in the present day. Whilst this is often difficult for modern Christians, the energy and the vitality of our forebears remain inspirational. The dynamism of their churches and the desire to be with people and share the faith confidently is sadly in stark contrast to the diffidence of many of us in the contemporary church. If nothing else, the reminder of these distinctive spiritualties which achieved so much in so short a time, should encourage us to recognise that all things are possible if 'the love of Christ urges us on'[64].

---

[64] 2 Corinthians 5:14.

Chapter Seven
The jewels of the crown

The revival and growth of the church from the Reformation to the beginning of the twentieth century encompasses many of the key spiritual traditions which contribute to the church as it is in our day. It is clear that there is much over the last five hundred years that has been deeply divisive. There are many events which reflect no credit upon the Christian church and seem to have little to do with the Gospel. The Archbishops of Canterbury and York reflected upon this bittersweet relationship of the modern churches with the Reformation, in a statement to mark the five hundredth anniversary of Martin Luther's *Ninety-five Theses*:

'The Reformation was a process of both renewal and division amongst Christians in Europe. In this Reformation Anniversary year, many Christians will want to give thanks for the great blessings they have received to which the Reformation directly contributed. Amongst much else these would include clear proclamation of the Gospel of grace, the availability of the Bible to all in their own language and the recognition of the calling of lay people to serve God in the world and in the church.

'Many will also remember the lasting damage done five centuries ago to the unity of the Church, in defiance of the clear command of Jesus Christ to unity in love. Those turbulent years saw Christian people pitted against each other, such that many suffered persecution and even death at the hands of others claiming to know the same Lord. A legacy of mistrust and competition would then accompany the astonishing global

*spread of Christianity in the centuries that followed. All this
leaves us much to ponder'.*[65]

For the Christians of the ecumenical county of Cumbria, the
distinctive spiritualties created in the crucible of the
Reformation still create problems and difficulties. Yet such is
the generosity of welcome modelled by both church leaders and
in local groups that often, the potential for division is overcome.
The problem of diversity, though, remains. For some, this
speaks of the breath of the church, but for others, this wideness
is a threat to orthodoxy. Recently, the inclusion of the Salvation
Army, together with the decision by the national URC to allow
same-sex marriages in their churches, has caused some disquiet
in a few Church of England parishes. Bishop James wrote to the
clergy of the Carlisle Diocese and expressed the need to accept
diversity as part of the greater missional effort and growing
together in faith:

*'Of course our unity includes a degree of diversity, and we are
embarking on this course of action with our eyes wide open. For
example, the Salvation Army does not have the Sacraments of
Baptism and Eucharist; Methodism does not approve
Episcopacy; and the URC General Assembly has recently
allowed local churches to conduct same-sex marriages if they
consider that to be theologically appropriate. My own position,
(like that of the Church of England) on all three of those issues
is clear, but in the interest of that unity for which Christ prayed,
that mission which he commended, and the furtherance of that
Kingdom which lay behind all his teaching, I am committed to*

---

[65] Extract from the Archbishops of Canterbury and York's joint
statement on the five hundredth anniversary of the Reformation
(January 17, 2017).

"good disagreement" and a focus on proclaiming the Gospel "in season and out of season"'.[66]

Whilst recognising the past hatreds and the schisms caused by the Reformation, it is possible at the same time to recognise the renewal of the church which was brought about through this great suffering. In this chapter, I am suggesting that there are aspects of the very distinctive spiritualties of various denominations that are a positive contribution to our journey together. They might be termed the 'Jewels in the Crown', and for Cumbria, they mark some of the most significant contributions the church has made over the last five hundred years.

Personal Piety
'Being desirous, through the Mercy of God, to please Him, for whom I am, and live, and who giveth me my Desires and Performance; and considering with myself, that the way to please him, is to feed my Flock diligent and faithfully, since our Saviour hath made the argument of a Pastor's love, I have resolved to set down the Form and Character of a true Pastor that I may have Mark to aim at: which also I will set as high as I can, since he shoots higher that threatens the Moon, than he that aims at a Tree'.[67]

George Herbert, writing in his notes to the reader in *The Country Parson*, evoking the personal piety of his age and his words from the early seventeenth century, could hardly have been written at any other time. His advice to the clergy which

---

[66] 'Letter to the Clergy' by Bishop James Newcome (November 22, 2016).
[67] *The Country Parson* by George Herbert, Leopold Classic Library, 2015 (p. 2).

was only published after his death in 1633, demonstrates his belief in the calling to live a holy life. Speaking of visiting the parish, he says of the minister,

'When he comes to any house, first he blesses it, and as he finds the persons of the house employed, so he forms his discourse. Those he finds religiously employed, he both commends them much, and furthers them when he is gone, in their employment; if he finds them reading, he furnishes them with good books; if curing poor people, he supplies them with recipes, and instructs them further in that skill, showing them how acceptable such works are to God'.[68]

Herbert's other great legacy to the church is the book of poems, *A Priest to the Temple*. Herbert was not alone in the seventeenth century in writing religious poetry to communicate the calling he found in the Gospel. Thomas Treherne was born three years after Herbert's death, and again, his writings were not published until after his death in 1674. His poetry and meditations reflect upon the Christian life, offering spiritual advice to the reader. His writings tell of his intimate relationship with God in prayer and his delight in the love which is personal to him. The last three verses of his poem 'Innocence' illustrate this theme:

'That prospect was the gate of Heav'n, that day
The ancient light of Eden did convey
Into my soul: I was an Adam there
A little Adam in a sphere.

'Of joys! O there my ravish'd sense
Was entertain'd in Paradise,
And had a sight of innocence

---

[68] Ibid., 22.

Which was beyond all bound and price.

'An antepast of Heaven sure!
I on the earth did reign;
Within, without me, all was pure;
I must become a child again'.[69]

Richard Baxter was a contemporary of Traherne and wrote 'The Saints Everlasting Rest' which was immensely popular throughout the Commonwealth during the years 1649–1660 and tells of the joys promised to the faithful man. Copies were distributed and read out loud to the troops of the New Model Army. Yet in 1660, Baxter became chaplain to Charles II before being thrown out in 1662 during the Great Ejection for refusing to swear allegiance to the Church of England as the only true church. There were many others who, in the seventeenth century, followed in the footsteps of Herbert, Traherne and Baxter, but of them all, Herbert remains the best known, and perhaps his most famous poem is the best expression of this personal piety:

'Love bade me welcome: yet my soul drew back,
Guilty of dust and sin.
But quick-ey'd Love, observing me grow slack
From my first entrance in,
Drew nearer to me, sweetly questioning,
If I lack'd anything.

'A guest, I answer'd, worthy to be here:
Love said, You shall be he.
I the unkind, ungrateful? Ah, my dear,
I cannot look on thee.

---

[69] 'Innocence' by Thomas Traherne, *Poems of Felicity.*

Growing Spirituality

Love took my hand, and smiling did reply,
Who made the eyes but I?

'Truth, Lord, but I have marr'd them: let my shame
Go where it doth deserve.
And know you not, says Love, who bore the blame?
My dear, then I will serve.
You must sit down, says Love, and taste my meat:
So I did sit and eat'.[70]

For Cumbria, the influence of George Fox was paramount.
Fox's experience of the 'inner light' and his rejection of the
Church of England's organised religion was rooted in a personal
relationship with the Lord Jesus Christ. For Fox, the call to be a
Christian was individual and could not be mediated through any
other person.

'These things I did not see by the help of man, nor by letter, but I
saw them in the light of the Lord Jesus Christ, and by his
immediate spirit and power, as did the holy men of God by
whom the Holy Scriptures were written'.[71]

John Wesley, in the eighteenth century, re-found his faith
through a personal experience of God. For Wesley, the Christian
life was a way of holiness, and he especially commended to his
societies, such as the one founded in Whitehaven, the writings
of William Law. Law's *A Serious Call to a Devout and Holy
Life* characterised religion through a series of stories satirising
the formality of the Church of England. Wesley wrote, 'The

---

[70] 'The Temple' by George Herbert, Rare Books Club (p. 44).
[71] 'The Key to the Faith and Practice of the Religious Society of
Friends', QuakersOnline (2007).

light flowed so mightly upon my soul that everything appeared in a new view'.

Under the revival of Methodism and the greater religious freedom of the nineteenth century, the evangelical revival was influencing many churches with a renewed understanding of the personal call of the Gospel. The Churches of Christ brought to Presbyterianism a priority to be rooted in the Bible. Primitive Methodist did much the same for the wider Methodist family of churches. The widely influential Baptist preacher Charles Spurgeon told his students: 'The most eloquent sermon you will ever preach is the walk to the pulpit'. In other ways, it was the holiness of living and devotion to the Bible that would make the preacher, not simply study. Again, for Spurgeon, prayer had to come from the heart and be sincere. 'True prayer is neither a mere mental exercise nor a vocal performance. It is a spiritual commerce with the Creator of heaven and earth'.

In the nineteenth century, though, the greater religious freedom saw also the development of Tractarianism which popularised piety rooted in the Catholic past of the church. John Henry Newman was the most famous and influential figure of this new movement. Originally, Newman was an evangelical, and like Wesley a century earlier, was greatly influenced by William Law. However, a tour of Italy and a visit to Rome in 1828 changed his views. On hearing John Keble's sermon in 1833 on 'National Apostasy', he became a leader of the newly named Oxford Movement. The Anglo-Catholic renewal which was to have such an influence upon the Victorian churches built in Cumbria, was rooted in a personal discipline of prayer and piety.

'God has created me to do Him some definite service. He has committed some work to me which He has not committed to another. I have my mission. I may never know it in this life, but I

shall be told it in the next. I am a link in a chain, a bond of connection between persons. He has not created me for naught. I shall do good; I shall do His work. I shall be an angel of peace, a preacher of truth in my own place, while not intending it if I do but keep His commandments. Therefore, I will trust Him, whatever I am, I can never be thrown away. If I am in sickness, my sickness may serve Him, in perplexity, my perplexity may serve Him. If I am in sorrow, my sorrow may serve Him. He does nothing in vain. He knows what He is about. He may take away my friends. He may throw me among strangers. He may make me feel desolate, make my spirits sink, hide my future from me. Still, He knows what He is about'.[72]

The populist Tracts of the movement covered many topics, but advice on prayer was most often the subject. Newman ended his life as a Roman Catholic cardinal, and his influence is across several denominations of the modern church. His vision of the church rooted in sacramental living which has, at its heart, a personal relationship within the Trinity, has influenced all our churches. The priority of Holy Communion in the main Protestant churches is part of his inescapable legacy. In the twentieth century, through the work of Evelyn Underhill and Gregory Dix, many came to understand the sacramental significance of personal prayer. Underhill summed this up well:

'Faith is not a refuge from reality. It is a demand that we face reality . . . The true subject matter of religion is not our own little souls, but the Eternal God and His whole mysterious purpose, and our solemn responsibility to Him'.[73]

---

[72] *John Henry Newman: Spiritual Writings* by John Ford, Orbis, 2012 (p. 45).
[73] *Practical Mysticism* by Evelyn Underhill, Stellar Editions, 2014 (p. 122).

Personal piety has a rich tradition and contains many different 'jewels of the church', and in seeking a growing spirituality in Cumbria, it is difficult to imagine that Christians of the future will not revisit these great teachers of the past.

Missionary Zeal

When the first Christians came to Cumbria, they were missionaries. 'England' was evangelised before it even assumed its name. By 685, the whole country was divided into dioceses, and the various nations were all Christian. This remained the de facto status of England until 1689, for just over a thousand years. Even when Henry VIII broke with Rome, there was still only one church in England. As the Protestant and Roman Catholic monarchs switched sides over the next century, and when there was no monarch after 1649, there was still only one church in England. In 1660, the monarchy was restored, and then in 1662, the Church of England became the only church officially authorised in England. The Act of Toleration in 1689 allowed some people to register in holding religious meetings that were outside the Church of England. Indeed, it's not really until 1829 that there was complete religious freedom in England. Therefore, the opportunity to be a missionary in Cumbria is a relatively recent circumstance; it has only been allowable in the last 180 years. This simple fact of our history is often overlooked. The church in England had no need to be missional in our own communities for so long that it is not in our blood, and often, it hasn't even entered our thinking.

If mission wasn't possible in Cumbria until the reign of Queen Victoria, where did all those missionaries go? The simple answer is 'somewhere else'! For nearly five hundred years, mission simply wasn't an option in Europe, but the beginning of the sixteenth century saw not only the Reformation but also opportunities for mission. In 1519, Hernando Cortés sailed for the new world with eleven ships, over five hundred soldiers, a hundred horses and four cannons (not the clerical kind). Their main sails were inscribed with the message: 'Brothers and companions, let us follow the Sign of the Cross with true faith, and in it, we shall conquer'. Cortés went to new world to bring Christianity and civilisation. He took with him brothers from the Mendicant Order whose vow committed them to relieve poverty and to educate. Cortés himself, though, had little interest in his slogan except the world 'conquer', and he saw the native populations as being less than human and therefore of no worth. The impact of the conquistadors was destructive both to the culture of the Aztecs and to the other nations of modern-day Mexico; it decimated the population through introducing diseases, to which there was no local resistance. The tactics of Cortés are significant for our understanding of mission, as the rest of European Christianity followed the example of Spain and sent their own would-be reformers around the world, propagating their own favoured brand of Christianity.

For missionaries from England and Scotland, the preferred destination in the sixteenth and seventeenth centuries was North America. King James used his new settlement of Jamestown, and others in New England, as a convenient way to be rid of the Border Reivers. As a result, many Cumbrian families 'volunteered' to colonise what would become the eastern United States, carrying with them their surnames that, in latter generations, became so familiar among them—the Armstrongs, Nixons and Kennedys. Among these colonists was John Cotton, who studied for fourteen years at Cambridge before becoming a parish priest in Lincolnshire for the next twenty years. However, he disliked the formality of the Church of England and would not wear any vestments. As a Puritan, he decided to leave England and work as a missionary for the Massachusetts Bay Colony in 1632. Cotton followed the example of the Mendicants in Mexico and sought to convert the local Algonquin tribe. Together with another Puritan, John Eliot (also a Reiver surname), they established one of the oldest missions in North America. Their example encouraged a small group of Quakers from North West England, who described themselves as 'publishers of truth' and established themselves in Boston, although they were unpopular with the other colonists.

Seeing the work done by the preachers expelled in 1662 in the North American colonies, the Church of England was keen to share in this mission. In 1701, the Society for the Propagation of the Gospel (SPG) was formed for this purpose. A few years later, the Wesley brothers were amongst some of the first Anglican missionaries in the North American colonies, but they were largely unsuccessful. Both John and Charles, though, were greatly influenced by the Protestant Moravian missionaries who notably lived among the Native Americans, especially the Cherokee nation. They were noted for their selfless work and schools, in turn inspiring the Baptist congregations in the colonies to join in their mission. The Wesleys weren't the only Anglicans inspired by the Moravians; George Whitefield, in seven visits between 1738 and 1770 to North America, spent most of his life travelling on horseback, preaching to anyone who would listen. Famously, in 1740, he rode from New York to Charleston. Whitefield was a passionate preacher who not only held his audiences 'in rapture' but also used the media of his time to publish his sermons. It is estimated that during his lifetime, over half of all the colonists read a sermon by Whitefield; such was his influence.

In 1799, the Evangelical revival of the Church of England inspired the Clapham Sect to establish the Church Missionary Society (CMS) which was founded at a meeting on April 12, 1799, with Charles Simeon, Henry Thornton and William

Growing Spirituality

Wilberforce all being present. CMS came about during the same decade as the Baptist Missionary and London Missionary Societies, and these three mission groups were to have an enormous impact during the nineteenth century. The Baptist Missionary Society was founded as a result of William Carey's preaching in Leicester. He put together many of his sermons into a book, *An Enquiry into the Obligation of Christians to use Means for the Conversion of the Heathen* which was widely distributed among many registered religious houses of dissenter congregations. Carey took himself to India with the East India Company; he studied Indian languages and eventually translated the Bible into thirty native languages, founded schools and campaigned for the abolition of widow-burning. His advice to new missionaries illustrates the meticulous care and sheer hard work demanded:

'The missionaries must be men of great piety, prudence, courage and forbearance; of undoubted orthodoxy in their sentiments, and must enter with all their hearts into the spirit of their mission; they must be willing to leave all the comforts of life behind them, and to encounter all the hardships of a torrid or a frigid climate, an uncomfortable manner of living, and every other inconvenience that can attend this undertaking.

'They must be very careful not to resent injuries which may be offered to them, nor to think highly of themselves, so as to despise the poor heathens, and by those means lay a foundation for their resentment, or rejection of the Gospel. They must take every opportunity of doing them good, and laboring, and travelling, night and day, they must instruct, exhort, and rebuke, with all long-suffering and anxious desire for them, and above

all, must be instant in prayer for the effusion of the Holy Spirit upon the people of their change'.[74]

The years following 1829 saw a huge change and expansion of missionary activity. Mission was now possible at home as well as elsewhere, and therefore, missionaries started to come into Cumbria from other parts of England. Those missionaries of the Evangelical revival, in the broadest terms, brought teaching based on a conservative interpretation of scripture. The Churches of God which were so fundamental in the story of the United Reformed Church, began a series of home churches and preaching conversion based on the Bible's literal truth. Mission was seen not just by evangelicals as the mark of true faith, but, after 1833, also by Anglo-Catholics. In 1857, the universities of Oxford, Cambridge, Durham and Trinity College Dublin set up the Universities' Mission to Central Africa (UMCA). They were inspired to do this through a lecture series that David Livingstone gave at the universities that year. Due to the ready supply of keen university students offering to be sent as missionaries, UMCA was one of the best resourced and supported Victorian societies. The religious revival of the 1870s and 1880s also saw young people offering their time and talents into 'settlements', living and working among the poorest parts of England. William Booth encouraged his followers to go and live among the poorest, in the same way the university students, who lived for a time in settlements, sought to offer their skills to alleviate poverty. The most famous of these, Toynbee Hall, was among the first in 1884, founded in Bethnal Green by Oxford University students. Whilst there is no record of any settlements in Cumbria, some of those in settlements did travel around poorer areas of heavy industry on 'one-off' missions.

---

[74] *An Enquiry into the Obligation of Christians to use Means for the Conversion of the Heathen* by William Carey.

Growing Spirituality

As well as the missional activity of the newly invigorated denominations, there were increasing numbers of missionaries from abroad. Most famous of these were the American Moody and Sankey missions, named after the most charismatic preachers of their day. D. L. Moody and I. D. Sankey drew tens of thousands to hear them, including, in 1875 at Islington, the young organist William Carlile, who went on to found the Church Army. Moody and Sankey included popular music, like the Wesleys, over a century before and similar to the Salvation Army. Among the songs and hymns they introduced are many of our much loved Christmas carols, such as 'Away in a Manger' and 'O Little Town of Bethlehem'. This newly missional activity also saw old religious societies, such as the Franciscans, becoming more active; the introduction of the Third Order into Cumbria came at the end of the nineteenth century, although the tertiary order dates back to the thirteenth century. Even in the twentieth century, the Edwardian Church saw renewed energy in mission; this was the high point of the number of clergy in England and overseas missions. The Order of the Good Shepherd (OGS) formed in Cambridge in 1913 among a group of university chaplains to create a fellowship of worker priests, following a simple rule which called its members to keep to a daily Eucharist, private prayer and saying the Office, together with faithful stewardship of talents and personal resources. The most famous members of the OGS were mainly theologians and church academics; however, as an order, it embraced both the liberal Alec Vidler and conservative Eric Mascall.

The riches of the missionary zeal of the churches and individual Christians over the last two hundred years are part of the treasure of our heritage. This chapter has simply nodded in the general direction of the great teachers and activists of the church. Though it is their vitality which is the most remarkable to us, they lived and breathed God's mission, often without thought for their own health and well-being; they gave every day to the service of Christ. It is awe-inspiring to see all that they achieved in faith in just a few generations. In our day, we can be encouraged by their examples; we face great difficulties, but rarely do we face our challenges with the same faith as our predecessors. Most of all their hard work should humble us; they gave everything they had, every ounce of effort, to proclaim the Gospel.

SECTION C
Journeying Together

In this third section, everything is drawn together and the
question is asked, is the future simply an extension of our past?
If not, then what does the future hold? At the 2016 Clergy Day
in Cumbria, Steve Hollinghurst quoted Vincent Donovan's
saying of modern mission:

*'Do not try to call them back to where they were, and do not try
to call them to where you are, beautiful as that place may seem
to you. You must have the courage to go with them to a place
neither you nor they have been before'.*[75]

It is self-evident that both the Diocesan strategy, 'Growing
Disciples', and the 'God for All' ecumenical strategy are taking
the churches to a new place. The rest of this book attempts to
put this in the context of our common shared and divided past to
ask what is familiar and what isn't. Finally, we pause for a
reflection on what this journey together might offer in the way
of hope to others and ourselves.

Chapter 8 looks at our understanding of spirituality and how
prayer, in all its forms, undergirds everything.

Chapter 9 discusses the nature of community in relation to our
contemporary missional intent and asks why this might be
important.

Chapter 10 takes a step back to look at the significance of this
time and suggests a parable of hope.

---

[75] *Christianity Re-discovered* by Vincent Donovan, SCM,
London, 2001 (p. 2).

Vincent Donovan, in his 2001 book *Christianity Re-discovered*, said that we need courage in being missional to go to a place we have never been before. This, in a nutshell, is our problem. We lack confidence and the courage to imagine not simply the church as being different, but also ourselves as being changed. Only transformational change will be sufficient to bring about the impact the Mission Communities need to make. In the first six years of the Ecumenical county, our momentum of change has been slowed and checked by the need to maintain the present way of being a church. Some, I'm sure, believe that they can see their time out, and it will then be someone else's problem. This is a corrosive attitude and saps the vibrancy needed to reimagine our future. So what is needed? The previous seven chapters of this book are about prayer. Prayer gave our predecessors the confidence to establish the church. Prayer sustained them in faith. Prayer motivated their extraordinary missionary zeal. Prayer is the key.

What, though, is prayer? In our day, many people speak of being spiritual but not being religious. Many reports show that well over 60 percent of the population is interested in spirituality; many of those people pray. However, fewer than 10 percent of this same group sees the church as having any relevance to them. What's gone wrong? Given the rich resources of prayer and spirituality outlined in the previous seven chapters, it is incredible that this group is not flocking to us. So what are we doing wrong? Or indeed, what are we not doing right?

Do you pray? It's rare we ask this question directly. A recent survey of a sample of Anglican clergy, conducted anonymously, shows that the majority spend less than three minutes a day praying. Whilst this survey may or may not be accurate, it does point to the undeniable fact about our modern churches that prayer isn't seen as the priority. Do Christians live prayerful lives? Does prayer guide and sustain us in our daily living, in our homes, in our work and most of all in our relationships? Even a causal assessment of the state of our churches and society suggests that we don't pray enough.

'Christians cannot play for safety, and those who are held by God can afford to be daring'.[76]

In writing these words, Dean Gonville ffrench-Beytagh spoke from personal experience, having being exiled from South Africa for his views on apartheid. He saw the need for courage and risk-taking more clearly than many of us.

'It is possible to serve Christ wherever you are and whatever your work happens to be. Social workers and clergy and teachers are not doing a more "Christian" job than bus conductors or civil servants or bricklayers—in fact they may have a softer option. It can be most terrifyingly difficult to learn to find meaning in life and to see God and serve him when you are living and working in the greed and pressure and ugliness of industrial and commercial life'.[77]

All Christians have a calling to mission, and yet we are so often tentative and diffident. Why is that? Is it because so many of us in our lives are not rooted in a loving relationship of prayer? Scripture tells us: *'Always be ready to make your defence to anyone who demands from you an account of the hope that is in*

---

[76] Work in Worship by Cameron Butland, Hodder and Stoughton, Oxford, 1985 (p. 89).
[77] Ibid., 90.

you'.[78] Yet how can we give an account of something we don't know for ourselves?

Christian spirituality

What is spirituality? What gives us the ground to speak to others about what we believe? Spirituality itself is 'how we believe'. There are, of course, in our modern culture, endless forms of spirituality which devalue this word. It is difficult to define. Many dictionaries can only explain spirituality in negative terms: 'everything that is not physical matter',(*Oxford English Dictionary*). Christians, of course, can be much more positive. We understand spirituality as being rooted in scripture.

In the book of Genesis, we are told that 'a wind from God swept over the face of the waters'[79]. It is this wind that comes before the words 'Let there be light'. The Hebrew word that is translated as 'wind' in this verse is *ruach*. In many English translations, this is called 'wind', but 'breathe' or 'spirit' are equally appropriate. Spirituality is therefore as wide as our understanding of anything that is 'spirit-filled'. Ezekiel, the prophet, is asked whether the valley of dry bones can live. The answer he gives is that they can only come alive again if the *ruach* blows through them. In the Gospels, we are told by Jesus that the meaning of our lives is to become alive in God's love: 'I have come that you may have life, life in all its fullness'[80]. The Greek word for spirit in the New Testament is *pneuma*. Bishop John V Taylor suggested that both *rauch* and *pneuma* should be translated not as wind, breathe or spirit, but rather, as *aliveness*. Therefore, a spiritual person is one through who the spirit lives,

---

[78] 1 Peter 3:15.
[79] Genesis 1:2.
[80] John 10:10.

who brings to life in themselves and in the people they influence and the gifts of God's spirit.

Christian spirituality is about being alive. It is about affirming the goodness of God in the world around us. It is about seeing in our human relationships the relationship of love that we have with God in Jesus Christ. Those who are spirit-filled live life most fully. St. Antony of Egypt understood this in the fourth century, as Christianity became a fashionable religion. He 'retreated' to the desert, after the example of Jesus in prayer, to live life fully in God's presence through creation. The great spiritual teachers of the church have followed St. Antony's example down the centuries. Those who first established the faith in Britain consciously followed St. Antony's example— Ninian, Patrick, Mungo, Dewi, Columcille, Brigid, Oswald, Aidan, Hilda, Cuthbert and Bega; the founding saints of the fifth to seventh centuries prayed through creation. Spirit-filled and spirit-led, they gave the example to those who followed. They saw the Trinity not as a doctrine but rather a framework through which the Spirit worked in their lives. Spirituality was not an intellectual construct but, rather, about the nourishment of their souls.

Spirituality, therefore, is a way to describe our personal loving relationship with God which animates us. Some of the greatest spiritual teachers of the Western church—Augustine, Benedict, Francis and Clare of Assisi—teach us that each one of us is called to live every moment of our lives in the presence of the living God. Nothing is separated from the presence of God. Rather, our lives are a journey of coming to know that loving relationship more fully and completely. The medieval mystics experienced this divine love, and their writings have influenced Christians ever since—Teresa of Avila, John of the Cross, Julian of Norwich and many others. In the Reformation, the splits of the church gave us new words to describe spirituality. Devotion and piety were seen as a more personal response, as contrasted with the remoteness of the divine through the doctrines of the church. At the same time, Ignatius of Loyola gave Christians exercises which helped focus the rituals of a formal religion into a personal encounter with God. The revivalist movements of the Protestant churches in the centuries have followed, notably through the Wesley brothers, the Evangelicals, Oxford Movement and the charismatic free-spirited communities. All of these have recycled, generation upon generation, the quest for an authentic spirituality that is both spirit-led and spirit-filled.

In our day and age, we are fortunate to have a very rich tradition of spirituality. We can draw upon a huge diversity of experience. We have a treasury of modern writers who are helping many to rediscover the richness of spirituality. Thomas Merton, Brother Roger, Mother Theresa, John Main, Thomas Keating, John O'Donohue, Matthew Fox, Richard Rohr and Laurence Freeman are just some of the contemporary Christians who have rekindled interest in spirituality. Sister Annmarie Stuart gave the members of the first 'Nourishing the Soul' course in Cumbria the following definition of spirituality, and it is hard to think of a better expression:

'Spirituality concerns the love-relationship with the Living God which gives life, animates our beings, bringing our religious faith and practice to life. It awakens our capacity to savour everything with which the Lord has endowed us as individual human beings, in community, and face all the circumstances of our lives together with the beauty that surrounds us'.

What is prayer?

If Christian spirituality is about the way in which believe and are rooted in our relationship with God, how do we express this in our prayer?

There are two classical categories of prayer, 'cataphatic' and 'apophatic'. We are very familiar with some forms of cataphatic prayer, as this is the basis for our popular understanding of what it means to pray. Literally, cataphatic means to pray using everything—that is, words, thoughts, images and physical items. So we know that it is helpful to light a candle to focus our prayer, our churches, to a greater or lesser degree, follow a pattern of words, and we use certain actions to assume an attitude of prayer. Kneeling, putting our hands together, bowing our heads, making the sign of the cross—these are all the actions of cataphatic prayer. Using rosary beads, incense, vestments, and processing the Bible—these are all actions in formal traditional Catholic liturgies, but in attention, they are no different from the rituals of Protestant worship. The band playing Christian songs before the service time, the centrality of the bible readings, the thoughtful sermon, the biblical exposition, the familiar pattern of a time of praise songs and the recurrent themes of extemporary prayer are all forms of cataphatic prayer. In the public worship of our churches, the causal worshipper might be forgiven for thinking that prayer is simply intercessory. Much of our time of prayer can be best described as praying 'for' or 'about'. Indeed, it is often unclear what is the purpose of intercessory prayer; sometimes, it feels like a weekly briefing report to the Holy Spirit. In this sense, the predominance of intercessory prayer unbalances our worship and gives the wrong teaching about how to pray. Praying so often, we understand, is about saying someone else's words and constantly asking for things. Rather, Cranmer knew in putting together his various prayer books that cataphatic prayer has four equal balancing types—Confession, Thanksgiving, Intercession and Praise. Each type is equally important and is needed to act as a corrective to the other forms.

The problem, though, with cataphatic prayer is that if we pray only in this way, it is easy to think that prayer is something that we do rather than the truth which is that prayer is a relationship. Apophatic prayer literally means 'prayer with no external focus or stimulus'. It is the form of prayer, though which understands the Christian to be in a relationship with God through the power of the Spirit and focused on the person of Jesus. John Main tells us how we enter into this relationship each day:

'The qualities we need in this fundamental encounter between ourselves and the ground of our being are attentiveness and receptivity. In order to realize our complete incorporation with the Word, we have not only to listen to its silence, the silence within us, but also to allow the cycle of its life to be completed in us and to lead us into the depth of its silence. There in the silence of the Word we share His experience of hearing the word spoken by the Father'.[81]

John Main reminds us that prayer is about our relationship with God and the divine within us; it is about the formation of our discipleship, our journey of faith and the nourishment of our souls. Like any human relationship, the more time we spend in prayer, the more important and valuable it becomes in shaping our lives. In the same way as our relationships with our best friends suffer if we rarely contact them, if we are negligent in our prayer, our relationship with God can seem empty and dead. Imagine if we only communicated with our best friend one day a week, strictly for one hour, and that we did all the talking? Yet

---

[81] *Word into Silence* by John Main, Paulist Press, 1981 (p. 34).

Growing Spirituality

this is precisely the pattern of prayer for many faithful Christians. If we stop thinking that prayer is something we say occasionally and come to know it as the ground of our being, it can change our lives completely. If we are in a relationship with God, holding silence every day so that we can listen as well as know his sustaining love, then we will draw closer to Christians who achieved so much in previous generations.

Richard Rohr recognises the transformation that apophatic prayer can bring:

'God tries to first create a joyous yes inside you, far more than any kind of no. Then you have become God's full work of art, and for you, love is now stronger than death, and Christ is surely risen in you! Love and life have become the same thing'.[82]

Prayer is a life-giving relationship. This is one reason why the great teachers of prayer—Antony, Benedict, Augustine, Francis and Ignatius—remind us that we need a regular routine of prayer, in order that prayer ceases to be merely an action; rather, it becomes who we are: Christians living prayerfully. Bishop John Pritchard, in his excellent practical guide, *How to Pray*, points to the need for structure and discipline in order to build a prayerful relationship:

'The key is regularity. It doesn't matter whether our way of starting the day with God is a snatched greeting or an extended conversation—the important thing is that is that it becomes part of the choreography of the morning. We don't have to think each morning about whether we're to clean our teeth or not, because

---

[82] *Immortal Diamond* by Richard Rohr, SPCK, 2013 (p. 182).

it's part of the routine. We just do it, without agonizing, and we know we're the better for it. So with prayer'.[83]

Apophatic prayer is practiced in keeping silence. This is not the absence of anything else; rather, it is an attentive prayer, being fully present in the moment and not being distracted. Our modern lives are so busy and noisy that many people find apophatic prayer difficult. The daily entering into silent prayer, whilst a very simple practice, can seem like hard work; it can also be very unsettling. St. Francis describes the 'blessing of tears' that often accompanies beginning the practice of silent prayer. Once we realise in silence that God is within us, as well as around us, then it can be overwhelming, and tears follow. Some Christians are suspicious of apophatic prayer because it is outside their experience, and they recognise how vulnerable this form of prayer makes us by letting go of external stimuli. However, once we are able to be present in the moment, to let go all distractions, then we can become aware of the Spirit within us every moment of every day. Far from being narcissistic, this experience of our relationship with Christ leads us to look outward from ourselves, Thomas Keating's writing of *Centering Prayer* which is an apophatic form, explains this paradox:

'Centreing Prayer comes out of the life of God moving within us. It establishes us in a deepening relationship with Christ. Begun in Lectio Divina (the prayerful reading of Scripture) and other devotions and especially in the sacraments, our relationship with Christ moves to new depths and to new levels of intimacy as we grow in the practice of Centering Prayer. It is also ecclesial in its effects; that is, it bonds us with everyone else in the Mystical Body of Christ and indeed with the whole human

---

[83] *How to Pray* by John Pritchard, SPCK, 2011 (p. 82).

family. There is really no such thing as private prayer. We
cannot pray at this deep level without including everyone in the
human family, especially those in great need'. [84]

The effect of silent prayer is to suppress the ego and calm our
attitudes to one another, to become more compassionate and to
seek God's goodness in our human relationships. This
contemplative lifestyle is the fruit of this way of praying and is
transformative. John Main sums this up from a Benedictine
perspective:

'In meditation we develop our capacity to turn our whole being
toward the Other. We learn to let our neighbour be just as we
learn to let God be. We learn not to manipulate our neighbour
but rather to reverence them, to reverence their importance, the
wonder of their being; in other words, we learn to love them.
Because of this, prayer is the great school of community.
Christian community is in essence the experience of being held
in reverence by others and we in our turn reverencing them.
Even if our ideas, or principles clash, we are held in unison, in
dynamic equilibrium, by our mutual recognition of each other's
infinite livableness, importance and essential unique reality'. [85]

Cataphatic and apophatic prayer provide an important balance to
our spiritual life, and we can only grow spirituality if we have
this richness in our prayer life. As we grow spiritually in this
way, we will come to review each differently, as Keating and
Main remind us. Prayer is not for ourselves; it is about how, as
Christians, we live together as part of the church and, looking
outwards, how we perceive the rest of the world. As we grow

---

[84] *Intimacy with God* by Thomas Keating, Crossroad Publishing
Company, 2014 (p. 167–8).
[85] Main, op. cit., 78–79.

closer to Christ in this growing spirituality, we also grow closer
to one another and seek to find Christ in the world. The
Ecumenical county is therefore not seeking unity for its own
sake. It is about being more faithful as disciples; as a result, we
grow closer together. In turn, this makes us more mission-
intentional because we have greater respect for one another and
wish to share our passion that we have found in the life of the
Spirit. Prayer releases in us right attitudes to one another and
reveals to us our purpose as Christ's Body.

Growing spirituality, through an active and daily life of prayer,
is a truth that we have inherited from the spiritualties that we
bring into the Ecumenical county. We have a long heritage of
prayer: the founding saints Ninian, Patrick, Oswald, Aidan,
Hilda, Cuthbert, Herbert and Bega, who all knew this daily
practice; the Augustinians and Benedictines, who built their
great houses of prayer from Lanercost to Furness; the
Congregationalists and early dissenters, who found, in the Spirit,
a renewal of life; George Fox and John Wesley, who told others
of the path to holiness; the faithfulness of William Wilberforce,
in his great compassion for those in greatest need; John Henry
Newman and those Evangelicals who revived the faith in our
great cities; the compassion of William Booth and the great
Baptist preachers, such as Spurgeon; the Edwardian churchmen,
tireless in their energies; and so on, and so on—the list is
endless. All were united in this great truth that to grow in
spirituality is to be rooted in prayer. Only once we are grounded
in a daily living relationship of prayer can the Spirit transform
us into the people that we were created to be. Only through daily
prayer which is real and meaningful to us can we grow together
into communities which will be faithful witnesses to Christ.

Words are inadequate to proclaim this simple truth, but they are
all I have to share. Reading through what I have written, my

words seem shallow, and I find it difficult to express simply and clearly my meaning. Perhaps, though, this how it should be; we have long recognised in the Cumbria Ecumenical Spirituality Group that 'talking about' prayer doesn't convey its power and meaning. This is why all our courses offer 'the experience of prayer', and that alone can transform us, not words. As ever, John Main sums up this great truth better than I can in a few simple words:

"Our language is wholly inadequate and our thought too self-conscious to reflect the simplicity and actuality of this cycle. But it is not language or thought we need. We need only to become aware of the mystery within us, the silence in which we see our own soul". [86]

---

[86] Main, op. cit., 35.

Chapter Nine
Communities of prayer and action?

If Vincent Donovan is correct in that the growing spirituality of Cumbria will lead us all into a new place, then it's right to ask where we might be going. The last chapter reminded us that to grow, we need to be rooted in a lively prayer life. The story of faith over the last sixteen centuries has been about people who prayed and lived the risen life of Jesus. Donovan tells us we need courage to travel to this new place, and all the evidence suggests that at present, many of us lack the confidence to embrace our new future together. So how can we help one another?

The ecumenical county, since November 27, 2016, has been committed to a covenanted partnership. We are actively seeking to reshape our churches into thirty-five local partnerships, and we have named these Mission Communities. If prayer is vital to us in growing spirituality, in growing closer to Jesus and thereby to each other, what does this say about mission? The 'God for All' statement of the partner churches of the ecumenical county assumes three characteristics. Taking the original aim of the Diocese of Carlisle in 2010 to 'grow disciples', the ecumenical statement has added two others: 'to be present in every place' and 'to make Christ known to every person in Cumbria'. These are aspirational statements and, as such, will take a great deal of hard work and commitment, as well as courage.

Going forward together as Christians in Cumbria, we can simply say every Christian and every church will be:
- present in every place;
- passionate about faith; and,
- faithful witnesses to our faith.

Growing Spirituality

These three principles sum up the 'God for All' strategy and its straplines. We each live somewhere, so the church 'is present everywhere', and we each have a passion about our faith through which 'we can tell everyone in Cumbria about Jesus', and if we are present, offering a faithful witness, others will come to know Christ, and this will 'grow disciples'. Often, strategies can seem long-winded and wordy, but in essence, the 'God for All' strategy is incredibly simple and straightforward.

Whilst the strategy is simple, making it a reality is something different. In many ways, the biggest obstacle we have to overcome is our own inertia; we can easily see it as just one more thing to do instead of recognising that 'God for All' changes the context in which everything takes place. Our predecessors in faith faced as many challenges as us and even greater change. Significantly, the times and places where the church grew most quickly and made the biggest impact in our history were in situations when Christian communities flourished. The second most important part of our growing spirituality is our commitment to community.

The new monasticism
Without doubt, the most exciting developments in the Christian faith in the last eighty years around the world have been led by communities, and the revival in Christian communities in the twentieth century can be traced back to one person. Dietrich Bonhoeffer was born in Breslau, Germany on February 4, 1906. Dietrich was the son of a university professor and highly educated mother. He was one of eight children, having a twin sister, three other sisters and three brothers. He was brought up as Christian in a very liberal, humanitarian tradition. His father was a pioneer in psychiatry. He studied at Tubingen and Berlin Universities, and was influenced by Karl Barth, studying at the

Union Theological College in New York. In 1930, he became a lecturer in theology in Berlin.

After Hitler came to power in Germany in 1933, Bonhoeffer was expelled from Berlin University due to his outspoken views. Three years later, he established with Karl Barth and others the Confessing Church. He denounced, on the radio, the government as corrupt, Hitler as misleading the nation, and the churches for co-opting Nazi values. Leaving Germany to pastor a church in London, he got to know George Bell, who became a friend and a channel for the views of German opposition. He returned to Germany to found a series of illegal training colleges based on a community model. He was arrested in April 1943. One of his most important works was from this time: *Letters and Papers from Prison*. Implicated in the Von Staffenburg plot to assassinate Hitler, he was executed at Flossenburg two days before it was liberated by the Allies.

It is in Bonheoffer's writings, as well as the story of his life, that we are challenged by his compelling vision that for prayer to be real, it must give rise to action. 'Be doers of the word and not merely hearers'.[87] He lived in extraordinary times, and his story, together with his writings, provides a compelling, controversial and challenging witness.

Bonhoeffer's example and influence encouraged others to found non-denominational communities, the key marks being:
- Contemplative Prayer
- Communal living at peace with creation
- Focused on hospitality
- Engaged in issues of justice
- Working for reconciliation

---

[87]James 1:22.

Growing Spirituality

George MacLeod was one of those influenced by Bonheoffer, having met him in London. MacLeod founded the Iona Community in 1938; he himself had been profoundly affected by his experience of war. He served at Ypres and Passchendaele, experiencing firsthand the effects of mustard gas. He was awarded the Military Cross for bravery. His experiences led him to train for the ministry. He studied divinity at Edinburgh and in New York; upon returning to Scotland, he was invited to become an assistant at St. Giles Cathedral. During this period, his concern over the social inequality began to become increasingly prominent. In 1924, he was ordained as a minister, and became Padre of Toc H (Talbot House) in Scotland. Increasingly, though, he sought a community to express the compassion and challenge he found in the life of St. Columcille and in his understanding of the Gospel. He obtained permission to live at Iona with a small group, and together, they founded the Iona Community. He came also to have a prophetic voice on the need to have an environmental conscience in relation to the stewardship of creation.

Roger Schutz graduated in 1939 in Switzerland. The communities that Bonheoffer had created for the Confessing Church influenced him. Schutz and his fellow students met daily for prayer and bible study. It was the fall of France in May 1940 that convinced him and his friends to travel to the Vichy area to found a house of prayer to assist those most discouraged and in despair. The farm at Taizé was bought from the sale of the first community members' cars. A simple rule was established, and by the end of 1945, the community had seven brothers. During the war, the community worked to protect the local people from the Gestapo, being a refuge for those escaping from the Nazis, including many hundreds of Jews. From 1945, Taizé was renamed 'The Community of Reconciliation'.

Key to Bonheoffer's teaching was the link between 'prayer and action'. When Bonheoffer returned from the Unites States in 1939, he said,

'I shall have no right to participate in the reconstruction of Christian life in Germany after the war if I do not share the trials of this time with my people. Christians in Germany will face the terrible alternative of either willing the defeat of their nation in order that Christian civilization may survive, or willing the victory of their nation and thereby destroying civilization. I know which of those alternatives I must choose; but I cannot make this choice in security'.[88]

After his arrest, Bonheoffer wrote from prison: *'Our being Christians today will be limited to two things: praying and doing the just thing'.*[89] Restricted though he was in prison, he sought to live out his advice to others; as well as following a daily programme of prayer and silent contemplation, he also sought to do 'the just thing'. As a prisoner, he organised legal advice, collected money for fellow prisoners' families, arranged air raid procedure, acted as a medical assistant and refused to move to a more comfortable imprisonment in order to continue supporting others in the Gestapo prison at Tegel.

Bonhoeffer believed that there was a necessary balance between prayer and action. He identified four key issues:
- doing 'the just thing' keeps prayer from escaping into self-sufficient piety, and praying keeps doing 'the just thing' from self-righteousness;

---

[88] *Bonheoffer* by Eric Metaxes, Thomas Nelson, 2011, (p. 422).
[89] *Letters and Papers from Prison*, New York, Macmillan, 1972 (p. 294).

Growing Spirituality

- doing 'the just thing' keeps praying from hypocrisy, and praying keeps 'the just thing' from fanaticised ideology;
- doing 'the just thing' keeps praying from pessimism, and praying keeps 'the just thing' from resignation; and
- doing 'the just thing' keeps praying grounded in reality, and praying keeps doing 'the just thing' rooted in Gospel values.[90]

In the 1950s, both Taizé and Iona grew and flourished, becoming increasing influential. Pope John XXIII referred to Taizé as 'the springtime of the church'. Taizé became the first multidenominational community to include Roman Catholics. Iona inspired other communities and developed an international network of 'family groups' in which thousands follow a simple rule. The Northumbrian Community, Corrymeela and the Community of St. Hilda and St. Bede are all rooted in the original Iona community, but each has different areas of spiritual work.

The idea of communities of prayer has also flourished in new ways, following on from Bonheoffer's original vision. Bede Griffiths stayed at a Hindu ashram in the 1960s and, from 1968, founded his Christian ashram based on contemplative prayer and reconciliation between those of different faiths. The writings of Bede Griffiths have been very important in developing creation spirituality and mysticism of the new monasticism. Bede Griffiths, together with the Benedictine John Main, popularised Christian meditation, and John Main founded the World Community of Christian Meditation with Laurence Freeman in 1975 at Ealing Abbey.

---

[90] *The Cost of Discipleship*, SCM, 1964 (p. 46).

In the Unites States, Bonheoffer's example inspired the 'Simple Way' which began in Philadelphia in the 1970s. Jonathan Wilson, in his 1998 book, *Living Faithfully in a Fragmented World*, first suggested the term 'new monasticism'. Wilson pointed to the foundation of Bonheoffer and quoted him, saying:

'The restoration of the church will surely come from a new type of monasticism which has nothing in common with the old but a complete lack of compromise in a life lived in accordance with the Sermon on the Mount in the discipleship of Christ'.[91]

Wilson's daughter, Leah Wilson-Hartgrove, is one of the founders of Rutba House in 2004 in North Carolina that has devised the twelve principles of new monasticism, as follows:
- relocation to the 'abandoned places of Empire' (at the margins of society);
- sharing economic resources with fellow community members and the needy among us;
- hospitality to the stranger;
- lament for racial divisions within the church and our communities, combined with the active pursuit of a just reconciliation;
- humble submission to Christ's body, the Church;
- intentional formation in the way of Christ and the rule of the community;
- nurturing common life among members of an intentional community;
- support for celibate singles alongside monogamous married couples and their children;
- geographical proximity to community members who share a common rule of life;

---

[91] Metaxes, op. cit., 512.

- care for the plot of God's earth given to us, along with support of our local economies;
- peace-making in the midst of violence, and conflict resolution within communities along the lines of Matthew 18, 'unless you become like little children'; and
- commitment to a disciplined contemplative life.

New monasticism is growing across the world and is one of the most dynamic forms of growth in modern Christianity. Often, the communities sit alongside traditional denominations and are more attractive to those who are alienated by formal 'stuffy' church life. Communities are not limited to one style of churchmanship or denomination. Often, the communities overlap traditional boundaries in new and exciting ways.

Bonheoffer's legacy is profound for the modern church. His life and writings still make uncomfortable reading and challenge today's churches. Who knows what the modern church would have come to look like under his personal influence? In many ways, the community at Taizé and the struggle of eastern European churches, as well as the South African church and the liberation churches of South America, all represent his legacy. In the words of his godson Eberhard Bethage, '*he has become an inextinguishable sign of hope for oppressed people far beyond the borders of his own county*'[92].

Mission Communities
Cumbria's ecumenical programme, 'God for All', is focused around thirty-five communities. So what does Bonheoffer have to say to us? We witness the extraordinary growth of new monasticism both within the county and outside; what do the

---

[92] *Prayer and Righteous Action* by Eberhard Bethage

communities that have given life to our churches say to the new Mission Communities? Northumbria Community members, Iona Family Group members, the World Community of Christian Meditation members and Tertiary Franciscans all play significant leadership roles in each of the denominations that make up the ecumenical county, so what do the insights of new monasticism bring to Cumbria? Brother Roger gives us an idea of the influence the community can have in our renewal:

'By its very nature, community life turns towards both God and humanity. If it favoured purity of life, alone, it would be in danger of dying a slow death. It calls for the capacity to adapt to renewals. Being too far ahead of one's time leads to debility and fruitless argumentation. But lagging behind destroys the momentum of a life given for others. Today more than ever, when it is charged with the life-force proper to it, when it is filled with the freshness of brotherly love which is its distinctive feature, community life is like yeast at work in the dough. It contains explosive power. It can raise mountains of apathy and bring to men an irreplaceable quality of the presence of Christ'. [93]

Brother Roger's belief that communities of prayer 'contain explosive power' is refreshing for Cumbria's Mission Communities. It may also help to explain the phenomenal growth of Fresh Expressions (FXC) which is described as *'a fresh expression of church is a new gathering or network that engages mainly with people who have never been to church. There is no single model, but the emphasis is on starting something which is appropriate to its context, rather than*

---

[93] *Taizé: Brother Roger and His Community* by Rex Brico, Collins, London, 1978 (p. 169).

cloning something that works elsewhere[94]. Nationwide, there are about three thousand recognised FXCs, and for the Diocese of Cumbria, just over 10 percent of church attendance is in an FXC. The growth in the numbers and variety of FXCs is impressive. In Cumbria, they range from children's activities based on 'Messy Church', a church fellowship in a nursing home, a motor bikers fellowship, and a mountain-walking fellowship. Central to all FXCs is a sense of community, of people coming together in a place and, for a time, sharing a passion and for that to be blessed as a Christian gathering, including some worship. FXCs are as varied as the people who make them up and can be ongoing or short lived. These communities, though, are undoubtedly growing in importance for the churches and are growing disciples for Christ.

Often, it is assumed that an FXC might be 'a way into church' for new Christians. This is fundamentally wrong thinking, Tim Sumpter, in a helpful Grove booklet, *Freshly Expressed Church*, points that this is an unhelpful way to think of the impact of FXCs; he says,

'Convention might assume that new churches have much to learn from the experience of the older churches, and that such wisdom flows only in the one direction. My contention is that those of us in traditional churches have much to learn from the younger fresh expressions churches proliferating in the micro cultures of the contemporary United Kingdom'.[95]

---

[94] 'Fresh Expression of Church', https://www.freshexpressions.org.uk/about/whatis
[95] *Freshly Expressed Church; Lessons from Fresh Expressions for the Wider Church* by Tim Sumpter, Grove Books (Ev109), 2015 (p. 27).

In focusing all missional witness to be undertaken by ecumenical communities means that in Cumbria, there is great scope for the traditional churches to embrace the lessons being learnt from FXCs. Key to many FXCs are the idea of community forming around sharing meals. Sumpter again makes a simple but often overlooked assessment:

'Fresh expressions churches prioritise human relationships in the context of regularly sharing meals together. This may sound obvious, perhaps even a bit passé, but the connections being made around open meal tables with neighbours and friends (some of whom are living isolated and lonely lives) in homes and pubs, at barbeques and picnics, are truly profound. Underpinning all this, of course, is the commitment and sacrifice needed to invest time and energy in opening up one's home and extending one's pool of friends'.[96]

It is clear for us that whether it is in a Fresh Expression Church or in one of the forms of New Monasticism, creating Mission Communities is essential to the missional life of the Christian Gospel in Cumbria. Archbishop Rowan, in the foreword to 'Mission Shaped Church' in 2004, wrote,

'If church is what happens when people encounter the Risen Jesus and commit themselves to sustaining and deepening that encounter in their encounter with each other, there is plenty of theological room for diversity of rhythm and style, so long as we have ways of identifying the same living Christ at the heart of every expression of Christian life in common'.[97]

---

[96] Ibid., 6.
[97] *Mission-shaped Church* (GS 1523), CHP, London, 2014 (p. vii).

Growing Spirituality

It is this sense of coming together in community as we draw closer to Christ that is vital for understanding our growing spirituality and the journey that we are setting out upon. Bishop Graham Cray, who was the chair of the working party that wrote *Mission-shaped Church*, recognised this in his introduction in the same way that Vincent Donovan did five years later, that there is a need for missional churches to move in a new direction; he wrote,

'One of the central features of this report is the recognition that the changing nature of our missionary context requires a new inculturation of the Gospel within our society. The theology and practice of inculturation or contextualization is well established in the world church, but has received little attention for mission in the West. We have drawn on this tradition as a major resource'. [98]

By placing all our missional effort in the context of our communities, then the church will look very different from place to place. However, if our Mission Communities are the church in the way defined by Archbishop Rowan, then this doesn't matter; they are still places where Christ is encountered. If Bishop Graham is correct as well, then it will be in the Mission Community where Christians will engage in the local culture and context. Far from 'saving the traditional church', this will rather be a new church in a different place from where we have travelled, Tim Sumpter rightly points out that this will change our churches beyond recognition.

If community becomes the crucible for prayer to form the new church, then it is clear that denominationalism which was so important for defining spirituality over the last five hundred

---

[98] Ibid., xii.

years, is now becoming irrelevant. The vision of Dietrich Bonheoffer, George MacLeod, Brother Roger and so many who have followed in the ways of new monasticism and fresh expressions of church are leading all of us to a different future. Growing spirituality in communities of prayer and action seem to be our next step; this common spirituality has little place for denominations and inflexible church structures. Rather, we are called as pilgrimages to follow in the footsteps of Christ and to journey together. It is difficult to imagine that our children and grandchildren will have the patience for our stuffy church; rather, they will seek to know the life-giving truth of the Spirit and the power to transform life in the love of Jesus Christ.

Chapter Ten
Template of hope?

'All winter the land lay for dead:
Even lochs turned glazed eyes upwards,
Pale and smooth their stares.

'A whole month long the road snowed in:
Nights a crackling of frost and stars –
Waiting, watching, unsure and strange.

'Only somewhere on the wandering road
At last, this morning, a flock of snowdrops
Their white cries risen, their voices clear'.[99]

In late December 2010, temperatures across Cumbria were the lowest recorded for a generation. On December 23, -18.7°C was recorded. In Grasmere, the temperature was negative sixteen, and the church boiler froze. Although January 2011 was slightly warmer, an early snowfall, followed by freezing weather day and night, meant that the ground became an ice sheet. Along with many others, I struggled to keep my front path and pavement clear, and I well remember hitting the ice with a spade to break off pieces of ice an inch or more thick. By mid-January, many events had been cancelled because of the wintery conditions, and like everyone else, I was simply glad to be in the warmth of the indoors.

One day, as I walked out of my driveway and past the piles of ice, I noticed, by my gateway, poking through the ice were the first green tips of a snowdrop. I remember stopping and looking

---

[99] *Letting in the Light* by Kenneth Steven, SPCK, 2016 (p. 21).

in disbelief at this sight. I knew there was at least an inch of ice; how had the snowdrop made its way through?

It was a late spring in 2011, but temperatures improved in February, and all the bulbs flowered in their usual way, and, it being Grasmere, there were daffodils everywhere. However, I haven't been able to look at snowdrops in the same way again ever since, and each year, I look for the first signs of these flowers. Traditionally, snowdrops are known as 'Candlemas Bells', reminding us that they flower around February 2 each year. Candlemas, of course, is forty days after Christmas Day, and in the church's lectionary, it is the day when we stop looking backwards and start to look forward to Easter.

Kenneth Steven's poem 'Resurrection' which I have quoted in full at the beginning of this final chapter, is part of a new collection published in 2016. It is the perfect poem to finish this book, for it links the snowdrop with the hope of the resurrection. It is a fitting full stop for this short book. For we are only at the beginning of our journey together, we still have a long way to go over many generations. The future is beyond our horizon, and we can no more know what it will look like than the snowdrop can know the full flowering glory of summer.

Growing spirituality together within communities of prayer and action appears to be the means to travel to the new place that Vincent Donovan promises us, but what else does the ecumenical county offer? What will the Mission Community look like in Barrow, Whitehaven, Kendal, Keswick or in the many dispersed rural communities? Everyone is searching for certainty and answers to these kinds of questions. How can we commit ourselves to change when we don't know what its outcome will be? It may seem like a fair question, but of course, it is based on a mistaken assumption. Often, it is assumed that we can stay with the status quo, but unfortunately, we all know that we are living in such changing times that the status quo is an illusion. There is no fixed point in our modern churches that we can cling to; there is no institutional safety net. We need to venture out with confidence and courage, rooted in prayer and working together in community seeking God's guidance, walking in the footsteps of Christ.

Last November in Carlisle Cathedral, the churches of Cumbria crossed their own Rubicon. It marked a point of no return where intention changed into covenant partnership and we committed ourselves to journey together. Now, as we launch and commission our Mission Communities, we need to ask the right questions to move forward in each locality. This, though, is not the theme of this book; others need to ask the right questions to move forward as an ecumenical county. The snowdrop is the only answer at present to these questions, the smallest of flowers which offers the greatest hope.

We should now be done with looking backwards. We have travelled over sixteen centuries together in Cumbria, in the story of faith. It's a story of intense suffering and destruction, hatred and extreme violence—often done in the name of God. Yet it is also a story of immense courage and determination and, above all, of prayer and faithful communities. We can be inspired by the individuals and communities that have passed on to us their faith, but we can't return to their worlds. We need to recognise that this is our 'Candlemas moment', a time to stop looking back and thinking about how to maintain the past. Now is the time to be radical, to venture out with fresh hope, to play our part in God's mission in communities of prayer and action to see where that will lead us.

The 'God for All' statement agreed by the churches of Cumbria states,

'By 2020 every person in Cumbria of all ages and backgrounds will have had an opportunity to discover more of God and God's purpose for their lives, so that they will discover more of Jesus and the Good News and become followers of Jesus within a Christian community'.[100]

This huge aspiration needs thousands of small actions by individuals and local groups to become a reality. This will only happen if our churches and their congregations are transformed into places of lively prayer and active community. There is no shortcut to achieving this and no one way that is appropriate to all of Cumbria. The strategy, though, expresses in unequivocal terms the responsibility upon every member of every church to have this forward-looking purpose:

'Mission and outreach are the responsibility of all Christians and church communities, singly and together. There are, accordingly, several threads to our strategy for outreach:
  a) how, as individuals, we share our faith through events, encounters and opportunities of everyday life;
  b) as church communities, supporting, strengthening and innovating what our churches are already doing (or might be doing) to become more welcoming and draw people in;
  c) reaching out into our communities, circles of friendships and others to share the Good News outside the sphere of activity of the existing church, including 'fresh expressions', Messy Church, social and community action and Network Youth Church; and

---

[100] 'God for All' Summary, www.godforall.org

Growing Spirituality

d) *across all four denominations, Cumbria-wide marketing, initiatives and projects that stimulate people to think about where God is in their life, and encourage them to explore further'.*[101]

This strategy marks a huge change in our attitudes and expectations. This change has yet to become part of the DNA of our churches and Christians in Cumbria, but all of this takes time. The Declaration of Intent was only signed in 2011, and the Cumbria Covenanted Partnership in 2016; for the significance of these two statements to become a reality on the ground will take much longer than the ambitious date of 2020 suggests. There are encouraging signs and where the strategy has been embraced, progress is being made, yet there is still a huge task ahead.

The announcement of the first ecumenical county in 2011, though, has made an impact outside Cumbria. Many other groupings of churches have asked for representatives to come and speak about developments in the county. In 2013, I spoke at a gathering of denominational ecumenical officers at Church House Westminster. This was a nerve-racking occasion for me, as I could only imagine the serious theological questions that would be asked of me about the different ecclesiologies involved and the doctrinal implications of a shared mission and ministry. After I completed my presentation, questions were invited, and one hand shot up. I braced myself and then heard the words, 'It's not a question but a request; when can I move to Cumbria?' This has been my experience along with others from the coordinating group for the ecumenical county. Two of our church leaders addressed the national Churches in Britain and Ireland conference in Edinburgh last year, and they were greeted with similar enthusiasm. Others, of course, have followed in

---

[101] Ibid.

Cumbria's footsteps, but the other ecumenical county, Cornwall, is very different from our county. Other, more local coming togethers of churches are equally making huge impacts upon missional activity; a similar process has been undertaken by churches in Sheffield, but of course, their context is very different from ours. Cumbria's bold step in 2011 puts down a marker for the future; perhaps we might call it 'a template of hope'?

On November 27, 2016, four churches signed a letter of companionship to go with the signing of the covenant partnership. Whilst most of the attention has been given to the four denominations that are now actively engaged in forming Mission Communities, the other partner denominations shouldn't be overlooked. They, together with the various independent churches who are working locally with various congregations, make up the active membership of Christ's Body in Cumbria. The letter, signed by Bishop Michael of the Roman Catholic Diocese of Lancaster, Bill Bewley on behalf of the Religious Society of Friends, Reverend Andrew Dodd on behalf of the North West Baptist Association and the Reverend Dave Pitkeathly on behalf of the Church of Scotland, contains the following sentence:

'We also affirm our intention to go on praying and working, with all our fellow Christians, for the visible unity of the Church in the way Christ chooses, so that people may be led to love and serve God more and more'.[102]

---

[102] Letter to the members and representatives of the Church of England, Methodist Church, Salvation Army and United Reformed Church in Cumbria (November 27, 2016).

Growing Spirituality

We are a people of hope. Hope in the resurrection of our Lord and Saviour Jesus Christ. Hope in seeing God's mission established in our land. Hope in the power of the Spirit to breathe through us to bring new energy, confidence and vitality to the churches. Hope in God's world and that we are God's children. We might be a 'Candlemas' generation, destined to look forward without ever seeing the result of the steps we have taken, but that is our calling. We walk in hope, live in prayer and share faithfully in our common life together.

Cumbria Christian Timeline

Important Christian Dates	YEAR	Key Cumbria Dates
Edict of Milan	313	
St. Antony dies	356	
Canon of the Bible agreed	401	
	431	St. Ninian at Whithorn
	451	Latinus Stone
	461	St. Patrick dies
	553	St. Kentigern at Keswick
Death of St. Columcille at Iona	597	
	632	St. Oswald becomes King
	651	St. Aidan dies
Synod of Whitby	664	
	680	St. Hilda dies
	687	St. Cuthbert dies
	c.690	St. Bega dies
Venerable Bede dies	735	
Lindisfarne attacked by Norse	793	
	c.800	Urswick Pilgrimage Cross
	875	Travels of St. Cuthbert
King Athelstan's kingdom	937	
Edward the Confessor dies	1065	
	1069	'Harrying of the North'
	1133	Augustinians in Carlisle
	1147	Furness Abbey founded
Accession of Henry II	1154	
	1169	Lanercost Priory founded
	1242	Calder Abbey founded
Black Death	1349	
Henry VII becomes King	1485	
St. Ignatius born	1491	
Martin Luther 95 Articles	1507	
Henry VIII breaks with Rome	1534	
	1538	Monasteries dissolved
	1549	First Cranmer Prayer Book
Death of Cranmer	1556	
Elizabeth 1 becomes Queen	1558	
Parish Records and Poor Law	1563	
James I becomes King	1603	

Growing Spirituality

	1603	Reivers deported to America
English Civil War	1642	
Death of Charles I	1649	
	1652	George Fox 'inner light'
	1655	Swarthmoor Hall, Fox's home
Restoration of Charles II	1660	
Great Ejection	1662	
	1678	Hawkshead Hill Meeting built
Act of Toleration	1689	
	1709	First Baptists registered
Wesleys at Aldgate	1738	
	1749	Methodist Society at Whitehaven
John Wesley dies	1791	
Methodist New Connexion	1797	
Primitive Methodists	1811	
Catholic Emancipation	1829	
	1837	RC Church at Wigton
Thomas Mann census	1851	
Sankey & Moody's - first mission	1873	
Salvation Army	1878	
Evelyn Underhill Prayer	1928	
Methodist Church founded	1932	
German Confessing Church	1934	
WCC	1948	
URC formed	1972	
	1974	County of Cumbria
Churches of Christ in URC	1981	
	1999	Leaders millennium prayers
Scottish Congregationalist join URC	2000	
	2009	CESG formed
	2010	Growing Disciples Strategy
	2011	Declaration of Ecumenical County
	2014	God for All Strategy
	2016	Covenant Partnership signed by four denominations
	2017	CCL & Reach Team staffing complete

INDEX

Growing Spirituality